DBT EXPLAINED

DBT
EXPLAINED

An Introduction to Essential
Dialectical Behavior Therapy
Concepts, Practices, and Skills

Suzette Bray, LMFT

ROCKRIDGE
PRESS

Interior and Cover Designer: Catherine San Juan
Art Producer: Sue Bischofberger
Editor: Brian Sweeting
Production Editor: Jael Fogle
Production Manager: Martin Worthington

Author photo courtesy of Matt Marcheski Photography

Paperback ISBN: 978-1-63878-476-0
Ebook ISBN: 978-1-63878-664-1
R0

For my son, Finn,
and my clients current,
past, and future.

Contents

Introduction

This world has never been a particularly easy place, but the past few years have been especially challenging. Making a living, caring for ourselves and our family members, and paying the bills are all tough enough. But add to that the national struggle for equity and justice, deep political divisions, and public health emergencies, and we have a world in a near-constant state of dysregulation. Needless to say, we could all use a little advice to help keep us focused on our goals amid all the hurdles. For many people, dialectical behavior therapy, or DBT, can help them attain much-needed balance and stability, even as life continues to pose deeply challenging internal and external road-blocks to real or perceived existence.

DBT was created by Dr. Marsha Linehan as a treatment for people with chronic suicidal ideation, self-harm behaviors, and other challenges associated with borderline personality disorder (BPD). DBT is also used to treat many other mental health concerns, including bipolar disorder, binge eating, and substance abuse disorders. But be careful as you look over these disorders or think about others, and don't let the labels get in the way of thinking DBT can be helpful to you, your clients, or those you care about.

DBT skills are helpful for everyone, especially in tough times. It's a treatment that helps people regulate emotions while building a life that is worth living, that aligns with one's values, and is steeped in joy and connection. With such embraceable goals, it's no wonder DBT has become such an in-demand treatment. It is important to understand, however, that the current supply of trained DBT therapists does not yet meet the demand, and unsurprisingly, this shortage of providers is more severe in some parts of the country than others. In chapter 2 we'll talk about how to find expert DBT help.

This book will not make you an expert in DBT, even if you are a licensed therapist, but it is intended to equip you with the information you need to understand the basics of this therapeutic approach. DBT is a particularly complex treatment, and my aim is to provide an accessible overview. Consider this your travel guide to the DBT world.

Needless to say, I love DBT. I own and operate a DBT program and have been bringing people into the world of DBT every day for years. And that has helped them create enriching, satisfying, sometimes easier-to-navigate lives. When I think about how I have guided my clients and mentored my staff through this remarkably complicated treatment, I realize it's by breaking it down into "bite-size," easier-to-grasp layers, thus making it more manageable—sometimes even fun. That's how I hope you'll experience this book.

Consider me your affable guide and interpreter in this unfamiliar land—a place that, inevitably and with some work and focus, can potentially change your life.

How to Use This Book

In chapter 1, we will be looking at the origins of DBT. I'll explain just what DBT is, what a dialectical stance looks like, and how DBT helps with emotion dysregulation.

In chapter 2, we will look at the structure of DBT and how to set yourself up for success in this world.

Chapter 3 will introduce you to understanding emotions, why and how folks struggle with emotion regulation, and how emotions and behaviors are often intertwined.

In chapters 4 through 7, we will learn the key skills of four standard DBT skills modules: Mindfulness, Distress Tolerance, Emotion Regulation, and Interpersonal Effectiveness.

In chapter 8, we'll put it all together and practice how to track emotion-spurred urges and behaviors, as well as learn to master behavior and solution analysis.

That sounds like a lot, doesn't it? Well, it is kind of a lot. But I will provide lots of tips and help along the way, especially when things get rather detailed and are especially important to learn. Fortunately, you'll also see there are numerous elements of DBT that are fairly simple. For instance, many of the actual skills discussed in the Mindfulness, Distress Tolerance, Emotion Regulation, and Interpersonal Effectiveness modules are easy to understand and participate in.

At some point, you might even find yourself thinking, *How on earth could these help me? I have all kinds of problems, and you want me to use one of these skills? How is that supposed to fix everything?* While it's true that many of the skills are simple, success in mastering them is still up to you, and success takes *work*. Your willingness to apply them to the difficulties of every day and forgo hurtful behaviors is vital. Overcoming mood-dependent behavior—that's a fancy phrase for "I just don't want to use a skill right now, I want to do what I want to do!"—is the hard part.

I often tell clients entering our DBT programs to think of tackling DBT as though they are going to live in a place where absolutely no one speaks English. They must learn to use DBT principles and skills as their primary language to get what they want and need. They can no longer speak English—that's a metaphor for old, unhelpful, destructive behaviors that work to help them feel better in the short term but mess things up in the long term. Get it? English will no longer get the results they want. They can scream and shout as much as they like in English, but if no one speaks the language, those needs won't get met.

So, as you read this book, as much as you can, use the language immersion technique of DBT: Pretend you have moved to DBT world, where your one and only option is applying DBT principles and skills in each situation you encounter. Notice the impact being skillful has on your emotions, behaviors, and relationships. Take your time and tap your patience. Remember, you won't see huge improvements right away. The skills won't make you feel "better" all or even most of the time. They will, however, often help you keep from making things worse.

In this experiment, you might gain some insight into whether DBT might indeed be helpful for you, your loved one, or your clients. But remember, I'm not suggesting just test-driving a skill or two here and there; rather, we're talking about truly immersing yourself in the skills and principles. That means really being honest with yourself about this effort. Success in DBT takes true commitment and willingness.

If you struggle with emotion regulation, having a DBT therapist to mentor, motivate, cheerlead, and support you through rough patches is very helpful, and a DBT therapist can also play many other roles, as you will see! That said, sometimes it can be hard to find or afford a DBT therapist, so finding a DBT study buddy may help with motivation and inspiration.

An Important Safety Reminder

Many people who come to DBT are struggling with self-harming behaviors or suicidal thoughts. Don't take these issues lightly. Please seek professional help if you are in danger of harming yourself or others. Please remember that this book is absolutely not a substitute for expert DBT therapy. I and many other therapists are aware of the lack of trained DBT therapists in many areas of the country. While telehealth has eased this problem somewhat, if you struggle with severe emotion dysregulation and life-threatening and/or self-harming behaviors, please try to use this book in coordination with a well-trained DBT therapist, if possible. I also understand that cost can be a barrier to treatment and have included some self-help options in the Resources section (page 142).

CHAPTER 1

Where DBT Came From

In this chapter we'll look at the origins of DBT and its groundbreaking founder, Dr. Marsha Linehan. We will examine the idea of dialectics, the philosophy underpinning all of DBT. You'll also receive a brief introduction to the four skills modules of DBT. And, finally, we'll explore how DBT can help with emotion dysregulation that underlies many emotional health concerns.

DBT FAST FACTS:
SUPPORT FOR BEHAVIORAL HEALTH CONCERNS

DBT is a highly researched treatment. The following list, adapted from BehavioralTech.org (a Linehan-model DBT training organization), is a list of all the different behavioral health concerns that standard or adapted DBT helps as supported by at least one randomized controlled trial (RCT).

→ Borderline personality disorder, including:

- ▸ Suicidal and self-harming behavior
- ▸ Substance use disorder
- ▸ Post-traumatic stress disorder
- ▸ High irritability

→ Cluster B personality disorders

→ Self-harming individuals with personality disorder

→ Attention-deficit/hyperactivity disorder (ADHD)

→ PTSD related to childhood sexual abuse

→ Major depression, including:

- ▸ Treatment-resistant depression
- ▸ Older adults with chronic depression and one or more personality disorders

→ Bipolar disorder

→ Transdiagnostic emotion dysregulation

→ Suicidal and self-harming adolescents

→ Pre-adolescent children with severe emotional and behavioral dysregulation

→ Binge eating disorder; bulimia nervosa

WHAT IS DBT?

So what is DBT, anyway? It is an evidence-based mental health treatment developed by Dr. Marsha Linehan and her colleagues at the University of Washington. The efficacy of DBT is supported by extensive research about what works to help people overcome emotional pain.

At its heart, DBT is a type of cognitive behavioral therapy (CBT) combined with acceptance and mindfulness techniques.

But what does that really mean? Here's a super simplified explanation of CBT: If you change your thoughts and behaviors, your emotions will change. And when your emotions change, your thoughts and behaviors will change as a result. Clearly, the focus here is on change. The problem, however, is that some people tend to feel invalidated by that approach. They feel that the focus on behavior change overshadows the content and depth of their problems, and they are not fully understood or taken seriously by the very people who are trying to help them. (We'll talk more about validation in chapter 7, but for now, let's consider it a sense of feeling heard, accepted, and taken seriously.)

DBT, then, uses CBT and accounts for validation by including the following components:

→ Embracing acceptance

→ Aiming for mindfulness

→ Seeking validation of self and others

In DBT, the balance between acceptance and change is key. DBT treats emotion dysregulation and associated behaviors. When folks struggle to regulate their emotions, they can engage in behaviors that create obstacles that can prevent them from attaining the lives they want to live. At their worst, those behaviors can include suicide attempts, chronic suicidal ideation, and other self-destructive paths. That can be an extraordinarily hellish way of life for both the person experiencing them and the people who love them. DBT can be a way out of that hell.

THE ORIGINS OF DBT

You can't get us DBT folks to stop talking about Dr. Marsha Linehan. After all, she created a treatment that has helped hundreds of thousands of people all over the world. In 2011, *TIME* magazine called DBT one of the 100 most important science ideas of our time.

Originally, Dr. Linehan set out to create a behavior-based treatment for people who were suicidal and self-harming. These folks met the criteria for borderline personality disorder. However, as previously mentioned, the people she was treating did not feel validated when she tried behavioral, *change-oriented* therapy. They did not feel that she understood their pain and believed that she thought *they* were the problem.

She turned the tables on that challenge and switched over to *acceptance-oriented* therapy. As Dr. Linehan refined her treatment methods, those patients came to feel more understood and unconditionally accepted. But they were also adrift, lacking the skills or strategies to help themselves. And this is where Dr. Linehan had a brilliant idea. She began dancing between the opposites of acceptance and change, balancing change-oriented and acceptance-oriented techniques to offer the best of both worlds to clients who needed both in order to heal. In the therapy world, this balance of change and acceptance was revolutionary.

THE THEORY OF DIALECTICS

While Dr. Linehan developed her idea of balancing acceptance and change, she didn't yet know that there was a name for this embrace of opposites. "Dialectics" is a complex concept, one that is influential in scientific and philosophical thought. Dr. Linehan's executive assistant knew about dialectics because she was married to a philosopher who embraced the beliefs of Karl Marx—who just happened to play a big role in the creation of dialectical materialism—and explained the parallels. So Dr. Linehan started exploring this idea of tension between opposites, the idea that two seemingly contradictory positions can both be true and necessary at the very same time.

And so, acceptance and change became the opposites that coalesced into Dr. Linehan's developing approach to DBT. Next we'll cover the three basic elements of dialectics as they pertain to DBT.

The Interconnectedness of Everything

Everything is connected. Everything is interrelated. The air I breathe out will be breathed in by someone else. The ground I walk on is connected to a street that is connected to a mountain that is connected to the sky. My actions affect the actions of others, and their actions affect me. Separation between us is an illusion.

It's challenging to understand how we are connected to other beings, and in fact, the universe. But it can increase our understanding of our impact on others, and their impact on us. It also makes it easier for us to validate and understand, even if we don't agree, the viewpoints of others when we see us all as interconnected.

Reality Is Continuously Changing

Changes are constantly occurring everywhere. You are now older than you were when you started to read this sentence. Moments pass, the earth revolves around the sun, all over the planet things are shifting, evolving, changing. Your values and what is meaningful to you will also change over time, though generally not so swiftly. What was important to you when you were a child may not be as important now. Truth is constantly evolving, and what is true now may not be true even a moment from now. Reality is in constant flux. Embracing all this is important in DBT because it can remind us that although we might feel terrible now, that can (and almost certainly will) change.

Finding Truth in Opposites

Often, we get stuck in simplistic black-and-white, right-or-wrong thinking. We decide that there is only one side to a situation, no matter how complex the scenario may truly be. The beauty of dialectics is that we can learn to look at all sides of a situation and see more than just the good/bad of what we're experiencing. We can practice looking at all sides, as there is wisdom in being able to hold on to opposite perspectives at the same time. This helps us move away from extremes. Want to be better at solving problems? Developing this kind of flexibility can be key.

Here are some examples of dialectical statements that can be useful in learning DBT:

"This is hard . . . and it is more likely that I can solve this problem if I just keep trying."

"I understand how you might feel that way . . . but I feel another way about this issue."

"Sometimes I feel that people are unkind . . . even though at other times they can be very kind."

Contrast those to the non-dialectical statements below:

"This is too hard. I can't do it."

"You are always wrong and I am usually right. In fact, I am always right."

"People are just such jerks."

Imagine if these statements might impact your emotions differently than the original statements. Imagine how these statements might help shape your actions going forward.

The Four Skills Modules of DBT

One of the best-known aspects of DBT is the sizable skill set we begin to apply and develop as we learn more about it. The Adult DBT skills are comprised of four modules:

→ Mindfulness

→ Distress Tolerance

→ Emotion Regulation

→ Interpersonal Effectiveness

We'll be discussing them all here and in more detail farther along in this book. What you will notice is that two of the modules are acceptance-oriented and two of the modules are change-oriented. The main dialectic of DBT, change and acceptance, flows through the entire treatment.

Note: Teen DBT methodology includes an additional module called "Walking the Middle Path" that focuses on teaching further skills related to dialectical thinking, validation, and behaviorism. This module contains elements of both acceptance and change.

MINDFULNESS

Mindfulness is considered the core skill of DBT. Why is this? Think about this definition of mindfulness: purposefully paying attention to and accepting what is happening right now.

Using the skills of DBT requires mindfulness, because it's essential to respond to what is actually happening right now, not what we wish was happening or what we imagine will occur.

Mindfulness also plays a pivotal role in how we access Wise Mind, the state of mind in which we access our best selves and make our most successful choices. You'll learn more about mindfulness and Wise Mind in chapter 4.

Mindfulness skills are acceptance-oriented.

DISTRESS TOLERANCE

DBT distress-tolerance skills are broken up into two basic categories: crisis survival skills and radical acceptance.

Crisis survival skills? Think of these as the tools we use to navigate through bad situations, without making things even worse. They focus on:

→ Recognizing that we are at a level of distress that just might lead to instant choices that may not result in behaviors that are in line with our values and goals.

→ Choosing from a variety of skills to soothe and distract instead of acting immediately on our "crisis urges."

Radical acceptance, meanwhile, focuses on how to cope when we are confronted with distressing situations that we are unable to change.

Distress Tolerance skills are acceptance-oriented.

EMOTION REGULATION

The Emotion Regulation module helps with recognizing and labeling the ways we feel. Our goal is to learn to regulate our emotions and, over time, change how we respond to the situations we experience. We also aim to be more effective at encountering and responding to negative emotions. DBT therapists often tell their clients that success is not always about feeling *better*, but *getting better* at feeling. A key goal includes decreasing vulnerability to negative emotions and increasing positive events and experiences. In the end, that should increase positive emotions.

Emotion Regulation skills are change-oriented.

INTERPERSONAL EFFECTIVENESS

The Interpersonal Effectiveness module focuses on getting other people to do what you want them to do. Concurrently, we seek to maintain our relationships and self-respect. This module walks you through various skills that, while not totally guaranteed to get you what you want, will make it more likely that others will take your requests or your attempts to say "no" more seriously.

Interpersonal Effectiveness skills are change-oriented.

DBT IN ACTION: A CANDIDATE FOR DBT

A while back, Sandra called our DBT program because her previous therapist said that once-a-week therapy wasn't enough. Upon further questioning, Sandra said that she had been in therapy off and on "for most of her life." She found therapy "sometimes helpful, but usually not."

Sandra said that she often felt overwhelmed by her emotions. When upset or overwrought, she'd been accused of being dramatic and manipulative. As a result, Sandra said she often felt ashamed of her emotions and tried to avoid situations in which she might become upset. Sandra said she sometimes hits herself in the head or thinks about dying when she feels upset. Although she felt embarrassed to admit it, it made her feel better for a bit. Not surprisingly, she said she would like to stop hitting herself and thinking about ways to die. Her goal was to find ways to deal with her emotions. But she wondered if it was even possible because therapy hasn't worked out for her.

Sandra could be a great candidate for DBT. She struggles with regulating her emotions, and previous treatments just haven't been effective. Hitting herself and thinking about dying work to make her feel better very briefly (this is very common for some folks), but also creates shame and prevents her from focusing on long-term solutions and learning more effective ways to address her emotion dysregulation.

As a clinician, I am really glad she is here. DBT could be a great choice! If she is up for it, we will spend the next few sessions getting a full history of her concerns, engaging in behavioral chain analysis of why she hits herself and thinks about dying. We'll also map out expectations for DBT treatment so that she can make a fully informed decision about whether she would like to make the commitment.

HOW DBT CAN HELP WITH EMOTION DYSREGULATION

Have you ever found yourself feeling an emotion so strongly that you just couldn't control how you expressed it? For example:

→ You feel like you MUST go off on that person—they have it coming, you know—and just can't hold off?

→ Or you are so inconsolable that you just can't help but cry?

→ Or you are absolutely consumed by anxiety? So much so that you are frozen in place or can't stop moving?

Those are all examples of **emotion dysregulation** (we'll talk more about this in chapter 3).

For some people, this is a pretty rare thing. For others, it happens a lot. There are all kinds of reasons. Some people just have a higher level of emotional sensitivity. Some folks seem to be born with it. Others have a history of being invalidated for being emotionally sensitive, and that can make them even more emotionally sensitive. Some have a history of trauma. In any case, some people just have really, really big feelings. Sometimes these feelings come out in big, out-loud ways that others can see. Sometimes no one sees that you are in distress—but boy, do you know you are.

A big part of what DBT addresses is emotion regulation: our ability to determine which emotions we have, when we will have them, and how we express and experience them.

It is the antithesis of emotion dysregulation! You might think, *But I can't help how I feel!* And sometimes, you may absolutely not want to change how you feel, especially if you are feeling swell and things are fine. It's when you are bombarded with unwanted negative emotions that DBT can help you. That's when it's time to change unwanted emotions or effectively manage them so they aren't so threatening and disruptive.

Anger and Aggression

Research published in 2014 in *Aggression and Violent Behavior* has shown that there are potentially clinically significant results when using DBT to treat anger and aggression in various samples.

Intense irritability in borderline personality disorder (BPD) has been shown to be effectively treated in randomized controlled trials of DBT.

In 2014, use of DBT skills was also found to improve anger control, according to a study published in *Behaviour Research and Therapy*. DBT's focus on mindfulness and distress tolerance can help reduce urges to engage in verbal and physical aggression. And its focus on interpersonal effectiveness can help you communicate more assertively.

Anxiety and Depression

DBT is an evidence-based therapy for major depressive disorder, major depressive disorder in older adults, and treatment-resistant depression. It is also effective in treating anxiety symptoms. Why? Because difficulty regulating emotions and tolerating distress are at the heart of both disorders. Also, depression often includes rumination about the past, and anxiety often involves worry about the future. The present-focused nature of mindfulness assists with bringing thoughts into the now and reducing past-focused rumination and future-focused worry.

Borderline Personality Disorder

DBT is the most researched treatment for BPD and, of course, this was the population Dr. Marsha Linehan developed the treatment with. DBT's focus on mindfulness, distress tolerance, emotion regulation, interpersonal effectiveness, and a dialectical worldview strikes at the heart of the problems associated with the disorder: instability in interpersonal relationships, self-image, and emotion, as well as impulsive behaviors that can be self-destructive in nature. A 2015 research study published in *Borderline Personality Disorder and Emotion Dysregulation* indicated that 77 percent of people no longer met the criteria for BPD after a year of treatment with dialectical behavior therapy. Finding the right treatment can be crucial!

Post-Traumatic Stress Disorder

The trauma of witnessing distressing events can include intrusive memories, changes in physical and emotional reactions, negative changes in thinking and mood, and avoidance of thoughts and situations associated with the distressing event. Research published in 2010 in the *Journal of Traumatic Stress* demonstrates DBT can help people who are experiencing severe behavioral dyscontrol due to PTSD learn skills to manage these symptoms prior to entering other forms of trauma treatment.

Substance Abuse

When people struggle with drugs and alcohol because they lean on substances to help them regulate their emotions, DBT can be really helpful in teaching skills that can help them break that cycle. There are even distress tolerance skills for when the crisis is addiction. These include dialectical abstinence, which is making a plan for abstinence while at the same time planning for lapses, learning to replace addiction reinforcers with abstinence reinforcers, burning bridges to things and people that make your addiction possible, and finding alternate ways to rebel if your reasons for addictive behavior have an element of rebellion to them.

Other Difficulties

With DBT being effective for so many populations and mental health concerns, it's understandable why DBT is now being applied to all kinds of populations. DBT has been found to be evidence-based for suicidal and self-harming adolescents. DBT is also being offered in some schools as a regular part of the curriculum to teach life skills to the mainstream student population. A randomized controlled trial has shown DBT to be effective for children with severe emotional and behavioral dyscontrol, and DBT skills are being used to help folks dealing with the fear, sadness, and physical pain of cancer. Lady Gaga and Selena Gomez have gone public with how DBT has helped them. DBT is everywhere!

KEY TAKEAWAYS

We've already come a long way . . . and we still have a long way to go. Hey! That's a dialectical statement! And you've learned what that is, so you have already taken a big step in understanding the basics of DBT. As we move forward, it will be helpful to keep in mind:

→ Try as best you can to integrate DBT strategies, principles, and skills into your day-to-day life to get the most benefit. The more you "speak DBT," the more you will be able to regulate your emotions when necessary and behave in ways that allow you to act in accordance with your short- and long-term goals.

→ Striving for dialectical thinking allows you to better see the truth in a wider variety of viewpoints, thereby helping you glean a wider variety of choices for thought and behavior.

→ Start to notice times when you feel carried away by emotion and become dysregulated, or when you see others swept away by emotion. Take note of what is happening in the environment, the body sensations you feel, the actions you take, the thoughts you have, and the emotions you feel. This is great practice for starting to better identify emotions and will serve you in good stead as we move forward to other chapters.

I am so glad you are here and have joined me! Let's keep going!

CHAPTER 2

How DBT Works

Now that you've learned a bit about what DBT is, let's have a look at how it works. People who use DBT skills learn to steer clear of black-and-white, right-or-wrong, good-or-bad thinking; seek out the truth in opposing viewpoints; accept that change is constant; and acknowledge that everything in life is interconnected.

You've gotten a glimpse of that main dialectic of acceptance and change, and you've had a very brief introduction to the DBT skills modules, including mindfulness, distress tolerance, emotion regulation, and interpersonal effectiveness.

Now you'll learn how the treatment is designed. You'll see how it is intended to be delivered, and you'll see how it can change minds and responses and save lives.

DBT FAST FACTS:
HOW TO RESPOND TO PROBLEMS

In 2015, Dr. Marsha Linehan said you only have a few options when life presents you with problems: *solve the problem, help yourself feel better about the problem, learn to tolerate the problem, stay miserable, or make things worse.*

Solve the problem. Simply stated: fix it. Change the situation, leave the situation, get out of the situation, burn it down. Make it go away. Later on, in the Emotion Regulation and Interpersonal Effectiveness modules, you will learn DBT skills you can tap into specifically for problem solving.

Help yourself feel better about the problem. Feel less bothered by changing or regulating your emotional response. You'll learn more about this in the Emotion Regulation chapter.

Learn to tolerate the problem. Figure out how to tolerate the problem by embracing acceptance. This will be something you'll get more information about in chapter 4, when you learn about mindfulness, and in chapter 5, when we cover the Distress Tolerance module.

Stay miserable. We will skip this option in this book. This involves using no skills. We are all about being skillful.

Make things worse. Technically, this *is* an option, too, but we aren't going to waste any time on this one, either.

THE FOUR MODES OF THERAPY

A lot of therapists integrate "a little DBT" into their practice. And some do "DBT-informed" treatment, incorporating some of the DBT principles and strategies. But while DBT-informed treatment can be very helpful for some clients, it is important to recognize that research shows that comprehensive, or full-model, DBT is the most effective strategy, especially for clients who suffer with the most severe symptoms.

Providing comprehensive DBT that is faithful to the model requires providing four different components of DBT. These include individual therapy, group skills training, between-sessions skills coaching, and therapist consultation team meetings. This is DBT as Dr. Linehan and her team developed, researched, and refined it. When you are looking for comprehensive DBT for yourself, a loved one, or a client, you will want to find out whether the therapist or program has the ability to provide all of these components.

Individual Therapy

Individual therapy in DBT looks very different from traditional talk therapy.

Each week, the therapist reviews the client's diary card, on which the client tracks emotions, target behaviors, and the application and effectiveness of skills. If a client has engaged in a target behavior, the therapist and client engage in a behavior chain analysis, which is a detailed breakdown of all the vulnerabilities, events, thoughts, feelings, body sensations, actions, environmental factors, and consequences that occurred. The therapist and client work together to learn more about how this behavior occurred and what consequences keep this behavior in place.

Then, the client and therapist draw upon the skills learned in group sessions. Together, they create a solution analysis of skills for every link in the behavior chain to use next time (because there's always a next time).

When clients struggle with difficult behaviors that stem from emotion dysregulation, it often requires this type of intense examination. After all, if the problem was easy to solve, the client would likely have figured it out.

It is also important to note that individual therapy sessions are organized by hierarchy of target behaviors (behaviors to increase or reduce).

In any session, the most important target behaviors to address include:

→ Addressing suicidal behaviors and thoughts or any non-suicidal, self-injurious behaviors or urges.

→ Assessing behaviors that get in the way of actually doing the therapy. Included are arriving late to sessions, canceling appointments or other "therapy-interfering behaviors." (Therapy-interfering behaviors of the therapist are included in this target, too.)

→ Breaking down barriers to developing and maintaining a life worth living. These can include relationship issues, problems at work, or living arrangement issues.

→ Working together to increase skillful behavior.

Group Skills Training

Just like it sounds, group skills training is where folks work together to learn the skills of DBT.

The group is structured and psychoeducational. A typical skills-training group session lasts anywhere from 90 minutes to 2½ hours and is led by two group leaders.

A typical group starts with:

→ A mindfulness exercise

→ A homework review from the skill taught the previous week

→ The teaching of a new skill

Sharing in group is primarily about skills use and home-work (which is also all about skills use). Participants are asked not to discuss self-destructive behaviors. Instead, participants are asked to refer to these behaviors as "target behaviors" and are discouraged from discussing these behaviors outside of the group. Occasionally, because of scheduling or other reasons, programs will offer individual skills training sessions, but this is not the norm.

Between-Sessions Skills Coaching

Between-sessions, skills coaching is a crucial part of taking DBT skills out of the office and into real life. The idea here is that in regular therapy, calling a therapist between sessions is consid-ered unusual and only done under extreme circumstances. In DBT, however, calling a therapist between sessions is welcomed. It is considered an important part of the treatment, with some parameters in place.

Coaching calls are brief, about five to fifteen minutes in length. They focus on skills use, with possible exceptions of asking for validation, sharing good news, and repairing the relationship between the therapist and client if there has been a rupture.

Usually, therapists require that clients have already tried at least one skill to manage the situation before they call. Also, if the client calls, they are agreeing to be skillful and not engage in self-destructive behavior until the therapist can return the call (and that might be right away, or after quite some time, depend-ing on the therapist's commitments that day).

Therapist Consultation Team Meetings

One goal of the DBT consultation team is to assist therapists in providing the best possible treatment by helping one another stay motivated. It is a place where therapists can be vulnerable, request support, and receive positive reinforcement for effective behaviors and interventions.

The consultation team is also about increasing team members' capability in delivering quality DBT. Team members work together to monitor one another's interventions and treatment planning to make the treatment as effective and as close to DBT strategies and protocols as possible. Such a team is also considered "therapy for the therapist."

A therapist will ask for DBT skills coaching (just as clients are encouraged to ask) to manage their own emotions when they may be getting in the way of effective client care. For example, instead of saying, "My client is always late," I might say, "I find myself feeling annoyed when my client is late and could use some coaching about how to manage my annoyance. I could also use some suggestions for helping my client with time management."

THE FIVE FUNCTIONS OF TREATMENT

DBT is a comprehensive treatment. But what does that really mean?

As previously mentioned, DBT has four components of treatment, including individual therapy, group skills training, between-sessions skills coaching, and therapist consultation team meetings, all of which are required to make it "comprehensive" DBT. But those four components provide structure for five broad functions in treatment: increasing motivation to change, enhancing capabilities, generalizing from what's been learned in real life, structuring the environment, and increasing the therapist's motivation and competence.

Increasing Motivation to Change

Changing self-destructive habits, and the old behaviors that work well in the short term but not in the long term, takes hard work. Becoming discouraged is just par for the course.

Individual therapists can keep clients on track by providing reminders of a client's goals. The therapist and client also chart and review progress with behavior-tracking tools like a diary card.

Enhancing Capabilities

This is all about learning new sets of life skills that are primarily about regulating emotions, staying focused on the present moment, effectively tolerating distress, and being interpersonally effective. The skills are usually learned in the skills-training group sessions.

Generalizing What's Been Learned to Real Life

It's fine to learn DBT skills in a therapy office or in a Zoom room. But for those skills to be helpful, you need to be able to access them in the real world and in a wide variety of situations.

One way this can be accomplished is through practicing skills with homework assigned in skills-training group sessions. Another way is reaching out for between-sessions phone coaching.

Structuring the Environment

Structuring the environment in DBT is intended to support progress toward attaining goals. Sometimes this can be very concrete. For example, if you're trying to reduce candy eating, then keeping sweets out of the house is a great first step. Hanging around people who use DBT skills is also a good idea. Also effective: Telling others when you are trying to change behaviors so they can reinforce your efforts. This is often where loved ones can be really helpful by learning DBT skills themselves and providing validation and support.

Increasing the Therapist's Motivation and Competence

This is accomplished with the help of the therapist consultation. The therapist continues to stretch and hone their DBT skills, abilities, and adherence thorough interaction, validation, and support from a group of other DBT therapists. This helps the therapist avoid burnout and improve effectiveness.

DBT IN ACTION: ACCESSING RESOURCES

Ted struggles with managing his emotions, especially when things happen that make him angry. Sometimes he can punch walls, get into screaming matches, or even the occasional fistfight. It has resulted in the breakup of his marriage. And he doesn't get to see his kids nearly as often as he would like. He's not a big fan of therapy. He doesn't see how sitting around, talking about his problems, is likely to help. He has, however, heard about DBT. He is drawn to the pragmatic, skills-based nature of the treatment. Also, his sister is a therapist and says he really needs it. Even though it frustrates him to admit it, she probably knows what she's talking about.

Ted lives in a part of the country considered a "DBT desert," meaning there are not a lot of providers around. There is a DBT program about 150 miles away from where he lives. The good news is that the program offers telehealth. The bad news is that it has a months-long waiting list. The good news is that the waiting period will give Ted time to figure out how to pay for the services. The bad news is that Ted is struggling and needs some help now. Ted decides that the time before he can get into the program is going to pass anyway and that he might as well spend that time productively and get a head start on DBT. He also has access to low-cost therapy through a state-run program. He schedules an appointment and brings the book you are now reading to his first session.

SETTING YOURSELF
UP FOR SUCCESS

Setting yourself up to be successful in DBT requires being mindful of the main dialectic of DBT: acceptance and change.

The main reason you are reading this book is likely that you are looking for change. If you or a loved one are struggling with emotion regulation, you want things to change. And if you are a therapist, you are hoping to learn new skills and techniques to help your client change.

And I bet many people, including you, want that change to happen pretty darn quickly.

However, I encourage you to take things slowly and provide yourself with lots of praise and encouragement in your efforts. Integrating dialectical thinking into your day-to-day life will take time, as will becoming well-versed in the skills we'll cover in future chapters. Just like learning a new language, fluency in DBT takes time. For those who struggle with emotion regulation, participating in a comprehensive DBT program or working with a DBT therapist helps. For loved ones, please check out the Resources section on page 142 for books, websites, and courses that can guide you—and therapy for yourself isn't a bad idea. For therapists, DBT training and joining a consultation team can help speed the process considerably.

Creating a DBT Notebook

Remember going back to school with fresh new supplies? Setting up your notebook with brightly colored dividers? And the promise contained in the new school year? Setting up a DBT notebook can be a highly effective step in preparing to learn.

In chapters 4 through 7, you'll be learning a lot of skills. You may want to make reference sheets for those skills so that you can find them at a glance. In chapter 8, you will be learning to create diary cards as well as how to do behavior chains and solutions analysis. Having a place to store all of this information will be helpful as you progress on your DBT journey.

When to Seek Professional Guidance

DBT is divided into four stages of treatment.

In Stage 1, the client may be suicidal, engaging in self-harming behaviors, or lapsing into self-destructive or therapy-interfering habits such as skipping sessions or being habitually late. The client may be in chaotic, hurtful relationships or may be abusing substances.

The goal of Stage 1 is for the client to move from being out of control to achieving behavioral discipline. If you are in Stage 1, I strongly encourage you to work with a trained DBT therapist within a comprehensive program. If this is not available to you, perhaps a licensed therapist may be willing to learn DBT with this book and other resources as a guide (please see the Resources section of this book on page 142).

In Stage 2, a client has problematic behaviors under control, but they continue to suffer, often because of past trauma or invalidation. The goal of Stage 2 is to help the client move from a state of quiet desperation to one of full emotional experiencing. While it can be helpful to remain in comprehensive DBT while working through Stage 2, this stage can often be accomplished with a DBT-informed therapist. Some clients choose to do trauma work when they reach Stage 2, because they have learned enough skills by that time to manage emotions that can be brought up by their trauma triggers.

In Stage 3, the challenge is to learn to live: to define life goals, build self-respect, and find peace and happiness, and to lead a life of ordinary happiness and unhappiness.

In Stage 4, the goal is fulfillment or a sense of connectedness to a greater whole. In this stage, the goal of treatment is for the client to move from a sense of incompleteness toward a life that involves an ongoing capacity for joy and freedom. It is great to continue working with a therapist who is familiar with DBT who can continue to support your skills use while working through Stages 3 and 4, too, if you choose.

How to Find the Right DBT Clinician

Finding a trained DBT therapist can take some research and a bit of savvy. Many therapists do "a little DBT." Some of them, because they lack extensive training, may be unaware that with some clients who struggle with more intense emotion dysregulation, "a little DBT" may do more harm than good. Some folks who struggle with intense dysregulation have gone to a therapist who does DBT-lite, tried a skill or two, saw little effect, and then quit, thinking "DBT just doesn't work for me."

Some therapists and DBT programs have chosen to become certified in DBT. This is an excellent way of finding out whether or not your therapist has effective training. BehavioralTech.org has a list of certified and trained therapists, but this list is by no means comprehensive.

Certification takes a commitment of time and money. Many well-trained DBT therapists and excellent DBT programs have opted out of certification. If you aim to engage in comprehensive DBT, ask about a therapist and/or program's capability of delivering the four modes: individual training, group skills training, phone coaching, and therapist consultation team meetings.

KEY TAKEAWAYS

We've looked at the structure of DBT and how the five functions of treatment are accomplished through the four modes of therapy. Congratulations on becoming an educated consumer, loved one, and/or therapist and knowing what to look for.

As we move forward, it will be helpful to keep in mind:

→ There are only a few options when life presents us with a problem: solve the problem, feel better about the problem, tolerate the problem, stay miserable, or make things worse.

→ When looking for DBT, remember to find out if a therapist or program can provide all four modes of DBT therapy: individual therapy, group skills training, between-sessions skills coaching, and therapist consultation team meetings. If any of these four modes are missing, the treatment offered is not considered an evidence-based, comprehensive DBT program.

→ Even though you may be eager to learn DBT as quickly as possible, give yourself time. There's a lot to learn, with many new skills and new ways of thinking. And there can be a lot of old behaviors and assumptions to unlearn. So, be kind to yourself as you learn to thrive in this new world.

CHAPTER 3

Why Understanding Your Emotions Is Important

In this chapter we'll be looking at the problem of emotion dysregulation through the lens of DBT. And we'll introduce the theory of why emotion dysregulation occurs and how it becomes a problem for some people. You'll learn about accurate identification of emotions, and we'll discuss how behaviors and emotions are linked.

DBT FAST FACTS:
10 PRIMARY EMOTIONS

There is some disagreement among researchers about the number of basic, universal emotions, but Dr. Marsha Linehan focuses on ten primary emotions that are addressed in DBT. These include:

1. **Guilt.** A feeling of having done wrong or gone against your values.

2. **Shame.** Feelings of humiliation and embarrassment caused by behavior that makes you feel in danger of being different than, or ostracized by, others.

3. **Sadness.** Feelings of unhappiness, hurt, or sorrow.

4. **Love.** A feeling of affection, admiration, and tenderness.

5. **Jealousy.** The fear of losing something or someone deeply important to you.

6. **Envy.** A deep desire for something someone else has but you do not.

7. **Happiness.** A feeling of joy, pleasure, and contentment.

8. **Fear.** Feelings of anxiety, apprehension, nervousness, or panic.

9. **Disgust.** Feelings of revulsion, contempt, or loathing brought about by something offensive or distinctly unpleasant.

10. **Anger.** Feelings of annoyance, hostility, or outrage.

WHY PEOPLE STRUGGLE WITH EMOTION DYSREGULATION

Emotions, at the most basic level, are designed to keep us safe. They help us maneuver through our lives and determine how we respond to specific situations. They give us clues about who cares for us and who doesn't, whom to love, and whom to be wary of. Emotions help us decide how and when to react. When our safety becomes critical, the oldest part of our brain, the limbic system, goes into action. It swiftly scans for threats and signals us to fight, flee, or freeze. Its message: *This is dangerous, and we have to do something! Now!* But not every situation calls for fight, flight, or freeze. Our limbic system often hijacks our emotions in everyday life. Then we end up feeling anger or worry or anxiety that is out of proportion to the situation at hand. And that can create big problems. That's why learning to regulate emotions is so important.

Emotion dysregulation is a term used in the therapy world that refers to emotional responses that are more intense and last longer than desired (or are indicated by the situation). These stronger-than-needed responses can be hurtful to ourselves and others. They can lead to self-destructive behaviors, interfere with relationships, and get in the way of both long- and short-term goals.

The Biosocial Theory

The DBT **biosocial theory** asserts that some people come into the world genetically predisposed to feel things more strongly than others. These are our artists, our truth tellers, our passionate people of the world!

Without emotionally sensitive people, we wouldn't have great art, life-changing novels, or music that moves us to tears. Also, we probably wouldn't have activists and healers of all sorts.

Sometimes folks who are referred to DBT are worried that learning to manage their emotions will make them lose this sensitivity. Sometimes being so sensitive can feel like being naked in a world made of sandpaper. I often tell my clients that DBT skills are kind of like a parka—you can keep the sensitivity, because it is a great gift, but you can also get around in that big old sandpaper world without getting so scratched up.

Let's look at the biosocial theory in a bit more detail.

EMOTIONAL SENSITIVITY, HIGH REACTIVITY, SLOW RETURN TO BASELINE

The biological or "bio" part of the biosocial theory emphasizes that some people are just born more sensitive than others to emotional stimuli. They may:

→ Feel emotions more frequently than other people

→ Feel like emotions just happen, out of nowhere

→ Feel emotions more strongly and the emotions are more long-lasting

→ Have a hard time returning to baseline after experiencing an intense emotion

Some people with emotional sensitivity may also have a biological predisposition toward impulsivity. If they are impulsive, they may:

→ Have a hard time controlling behaviors, even though the behavior may cause problems

→ Feel like some behaviors come out of the blue

→ Have a hard time consistently achieving goals because moods get in the way

→ Struggle to control behaviors that go along with moods

THE INVALIDATING ENVIRONMENT

The social part of the biosocial theory is the idea that an invalidating and ineffective social environment can make it difficult to regulate emotions. The invalidating environment may:

→ Not pay attention to the emotions of the emotionally sensitive person and not help until that person's behaviors are out of control

→ Ask the emotionally sensitive person to change their emotional reactions without teaching them how

→ Show impatience or frustration with the emotions of the emotionally sensitive person

The invalidating environment, and the people in it, are generally not trying to harm, but instead:

→ People may not know how to help. They may not know how important validation is. (You'll learn more about validation in chapter 7.)

→ They may be struggling themselves. They may be overwhelmed, lacking in help, or be overworked.

→ There may be a poor temperamental fit between the emotionally sensitive person and the environment—i.e., they just "don't speak the same language."

So, the emotionally sensitive person in an invalidating environment comes to believe that their emotions are weird, and they aren't taught how to regulate them but only given help when the emotions are out of control.

THE TRANSACTION COUNTS

It is certainly not the intent of many loved ones to make things harder on those who are emotionally sensitive, but this message can be conveyed nonetheless, and the emotionally sensitive person may feel like their emotions just don't make sense.

In the *DBT Skills Training Manual*, Dr. Linehan discusses how some people are just born more emotionally sensitive, and the higher emotional sensitivity a child possesses, the greater the likelihood they will not be validated in their environment, which then leads to even greater emotionality. The transactions or interactions between the person and their social environment can help offset this discrepancy.

That's why it is so important for people who struggle with emotion dysregulation, their loved ones, and therapists to learn DBT skills, especially validation. It's vital that they get on the same page and create more validating environments for emotionally sensitive people.

Types of Emotion Dysregulation

Dr. Marsha Linehan notes in the *DBT Skills Training Manual* that people who struggle with regulating emotions tend to manifest these difficulties in five different areas of dysregulation, including emotional, interpersonal, self, cognitive, and behavioral. These areas of dysregulation are a reorganization of the *Diagnostic and Statistical Manual of Mental Disorders (DSM)* criteria for borderline personality disorder (BPD). Many people who benefit from DBT can find some symptoms they struggle with in one or more of these areas of dysregulation, whether or not they meet *DSM* criteria for BPD. Remember that DBT has expanded beyond treatment of BPD. While many mental health issues are characterized by some difficulty in regulating emotions, these areas of dysregulation do not have to be present for DBT to be helpful. Dr. Linehan notes that substance use disorders, eating disorders, and other destructive behaviors are often escapes from unbearable emotions. Dr. Linehan also reminds us that anxiety disorders and bipolar disorders are linked to emotion dysregulation.

EMOTIONAL

Dysregulation that is emotional in nature is a feeling of being controlled and overwhelmed by emotions. It's a feeling that emotions are out of control and they are intolerable. Often the emotions are strong, sudden, and rapidly changing. The behavior associated with these emotions is not consistent with the person's goals.

INTERPERSONAL

When interpersonal dysregulation is present, relationships can sometimes be stormy and chaotic. When things are great, they are really great. But when things go wrong, it feels like the relationship is broken beyond repair. For some people, there is an intense fear of being abandoned that sometimes results in behaviors that might even result in further abandonment. Examples of these behaviors can include excessive text messaging or phone calls, refusing to leave, or even pleading or clinging to someone when they request space.

SELF

Self-dysregulation can feel like a sense of emptiness, loneliness, boredom, or lack of a sense of self. Shifts in values, ideas, identity, and goals may occur, depending on whom one is around. People who struggle with self-dysregulation can look to others to try to fit in but often remain feeling alone and misunderstood.

COGNITIVE

Simply stated, cognitive dysregulation means experiencing problems in thinking. Many things are "black and white" or "all or nothing." This is targeted through dialectical thinking, as you read about in chapter 1. Another variety of cognitive dysregulation is feeling like you or the world around you isn't real. This is called dissociation. And finally, some folks can feel a sense of paranoia. These final two kinds are particularly prevalent when emotions are running high.

Behavioral dysregulation is the inability to control behaviors that are brought about by big emotions. As a response to emotional suffering, a person may have urges to self-harm or may engage in various impulsive behaviors such as drugs, alcohol, spending, gambling, eating binges, unsafe driving, or unsafe sex. People might make suicide attempts. They may also struggle with communicating their emotions in an effective way and make threats when trying to communicate how much pain they are in.

HOW TO RECOGNIZE YOUR FEELINGS

Recognizing emotions is a huge part of regulating them. But remember, some people have emotions that hit them like a ton of bricks, fast and hard, and they'd rather not feel them at all, so they tend to do things to avoid the feelings altogether. This is called emotional avoidance, and it is the driver behind many problematic behaviors that are treated by DBT. Dr. Marsha Linehan notes in the *DBT Skills Training Handbook* that DBT is not always about feeling better but getting better at feeling. That's what emotion regulation is: not feeling awesome all of the time but being able to feel emotions without getting completely rocked by them. Something to know is that recognizing and naming a feeling reduces its intensity. An emotion lasts only about ninety seconds unless we feed it, but not feeding it can be difficult.

Understanding Basic Emotions

Emotions are commonly called feelings. Why? Because we *feel* them. Body sensations are a component of emotions. If you scan your body, you can get a sense of the emotion you are feeling. Is your jaw clenched? Are your shoulders tense? Does your chest feel tight? Do you have butterflies in your stomach?

Emotions also have associated action urges. With fear, you may have the urge to avoid the situation or person you are afraid of. Anger may make you feel like lashing out verbally or physically. Shame may trigger the urge to hide. Jealousy may make you want to try to control another's behavior. Once we recognize the body sensations and the action urges, we can usually make a pretty good guess as to the emotion being felt. As I mention on page 88, just naming an emotion gives us a bit of space between it and ourselves so that we can think and use coping strategies rather than be completely carried away by it.

The Difference Between Primary and Secondary Emotions

A primary emotion is our immediate, first reaction to a given situation. A secondary emotion is most commonly our reaction to a primary emotion. Let's say I feel sad about something. For example, a friend canceled our plans for today. If I feel that feeling, it is going to last about ninety seconds. I may feel it again a few times throughout the day. If I feel it again without feeding it, I may feel it again for a few minutes each time. But, let's say, I start adding on my beliefs, judgments, and assumptions about what it means that I feel sad about my friend canceling our plans. Maybe I decide that feeling sad means I am headed for a major depressive episode. Maybe I start to think that my friend didn't want to spend time with me because I am always sad, and a downer, and no fun to be around, and she just couldn't stand to be with me today. Or, she's just my friend because she feels sorry for me. This, in turn, elicits the secondary emotion of shame. Now I can start thinking about all of the embarrassing things that have happened to me throughout my life and go into a complete shame spiral that can last days. As you can see, secondary emotions can cause big problems.

How Judgments Impact Your Emotions

The previous example demonstrated how important our self-judgments are in creating strong emotions. Judgments of other people, places, and things are equally impactful. We'll talk a bit more about judgments when we talk about mindfulness in chapter 4. Judgments are emotion generators. If we have positive judgments of something or someone, generally we have positive emotions about that something or someone. If we have negative judgments of something or someone, generally we have negative emotions. Remember when I talked about the limbic system seeing danger when there isn't any (page 33)? Especially when folks are emotionally sensitive, they can see danger and make judgments that people have a negative intent when that's not the case. This has strong negative impacts on relationships. When safety is important, making judgments is vital. But when loved ones are accused of ill intent in the heat of the moment, it is difficult for the relationship to recover. Becoming aware of the number of judgments we make in daily life can be a great first step in increasing emotional awareness and the ability to regulate. Aim for factually describing situations rather than using judgments.

DBT IN ACTION:
ADDRESSING SHAME AND SELF-HARM

When Taylor heard about the biosocial theory of DBT, she felt like it had been written just about her. She felt like her emotions and behaviors came out of nowhere, hit hard and fast, and kicked her to the curb. She was heartened by the idea that she wasn't the only one who experienced this. Taylor was fairly convinced that she wasn't going to be able to learn to regulate her emotions. Her experience was that her emotions just "happened."

Then she and her new DBT therapist started to pay attention to what happened before and after she engaged in behaviors that she later felt bad about. The first behavior they agreed to target was cutting. Taylor worked hard on her mindfulness skills in order to get better at recognizing changes in her emotional states and carefully recorded her self-harm urges and actions on her diary card.

Taylor and her therapist noticed that Taylor usually cut herself when she felt deep shame after assuming that someone had judged her. The cutting behavior worked in the moment to distract Taylor from the shame. But later, she would feel even more shame at having self-harmed. This all took a little while to figure out as Taylor often had a hard time remembering what had happened because of her high level of emotion. It can be hard to recall events that occur when we are distraught.

They stuck to it and were able to create a skills plan for Taylor to follow when she is in similar situations. Taylor was able to report at her last session that she had self-harm urges but used skills instead.

THE LINK BETWEEN EMOTIONS AND BEHAVIORS

We just spent some time talking about how emotions have associated action urges. Sometimes it makes sense to follow through with these urges. For example: If I feel a surge of love for my son, I follow through with the behavior of hugging him (unless it's in front of his friends, because he's 12).

In DBT, you will often hear problematic behaviors described as "mood-dependent." When someone engages in mood-dependent behavior, it means they are acting on the urges created by their emotions. So, when you direct an obscene gesture at the driver that pulled in front of you abruptly, you are engaging in mood-dependent behavior. It feels so justified and so good in the moment. But later, upon a bit of reflection, you may feel a bit guilty or ashamed, or even a bit scared. What if that driver had a gun and you triggered an eruption of road rage? This is the problem with mood-dependent behavior: We have the immediate reward of feeling something good (in this case, feeling justified and powerful in our expression of anger). This immediate reward makes it more likely that we will engage in this behavior again, even though it can be followed by the longer-lasting feelings of shame, guilt, and fear.

How Your Emotions Become Actions

At the beginning of DBT therapy, a main goal is identifying mood-dependent behaviors that get in the way of attaining a life worth living. We call these "target behaviors" because we want to target them in treatment. If someone has endured trauma, abuse, or invalidation, they can often be triggered emotionally by present experiences that feel similar to those previous events.

Once triggered by these experiences, a person who struggles with emotion dysregulation may be more likely to deal with those triggers by engaging in mood-dependent behavior, especially because, as you just learned, what happens immediately after the mood-dependent behavior can often reinforce the behavior and make it more likely to happen again. The mood-dependent behaviors that are life-threatening in nature, including self-harm behaviors, will be attended to first and will be included on the diary card for the client to track and the therapist to review each session. You'll learn more about diary cards in chapter 8.

Finding the Links Between Specific Behaviors and Reactions

Throughout treatment, the DBT therapist and client will carefully map out the links between specific behaviors and reactions. This is called a behavioral chain analysis. It aims for a complete picture of the events, including the client's thoughts, feelings, body sensations, actions, and things that occurred in the client's environment at the time of the target behavior. The client's vulnerabilities prior to the target behavior and the consequences of the target behavior are also examined. This helps the client and therapist gain a comprehensive understanding of the behavior and what elicits it. So often, when something we wish hadn't happened happens, we just don't want to think about it later. This is understandable. But this sort of intensive examination of the target behavior is vital in changing the behaviors with the application of DBT skills. The application of skills to a behavior chain is called solution analysis. You'll learn more about this in chapter 8.

KEY TAKEAWAYS

We've seen how emotions and behaviors walk hand in hand. And we've learned how emotion dysregulation can result in destructive behaviors. You've learned about the biosocial theory and types of emotion dysregulation. As we move forward, it will be helpful to keep in mind:

→ Emotional sensitivity is not always problematic. It is also a gift. Folks with emotional sensitivity are often compassionate, empathic, artistic, and passionate about causes.

→ Identifying and naming emotions can reduce their intensity. Reducing your judgments can also reduce the intensity of your emotions.

→ Start noticing the links between your emotions and behaviors you would like to change. Take notes about where you are, who was around, what you were think-ing and feeling, and your body's sensations to collect data about potential links.

CHAPTER 4

Understanding How Mindfulness Works

In this chapter we will be looking at what mindfulness is and how it is practiced in DBT. We will examine the concept of the three states of mind and learn about how to achieve Wise Mind, the state of mind where we can best access our inner wisdom. You'll learn about basic mindfulness skills and how to go about starting your own mindfulness practice. Mindfulness is pretty popular these days, so I bet you've had some exposure to it, but here you can learn about how it applies to DBT.

DBT FAST FACTS: MINDFULNESS IN FOUR STEPS

1. Choose something to do mindfully: pet your cat, breathe in and out, eat an ice cream cone, take a bath

2. Focus on the activity: focus on being in the present moment while doing the activity

3. Notice when your attention wanders; it's normal for attention to wander. Our brain thinks and thinks and thinks and thinks. Just notice when it does.

4. Gently bring your attention back: after you have noticed that you are not paying attention to the activity, gently, without judging yourself (or your brain), bring your attention back to the task at hand.

That's it! Welcome to mindfulness. Read on to learn more.

WHAT IS MINDFULNESS?

According to the *DBT Skills Training Handbook*, mindfulness is the core skill of DBT. In general, we can define mindfulness as being aware in the present moment, on purpose, without judgment, and without holding on to the moment. The idea is being present to the experience of each new moment as it is happening instead of as we wish it was happening.

Mindfulness is the opposite of being on autopilot. When you're on autopilot, you're doing things habitually, by rote, often without thinking. Have you ever driven to work without remembering how you got there? That's an example of being on autopilot. You weren't thinking of turning the key in the ignition and braking and pressing the accelerator. You just did all the things and found yourself at work.

Doing things on autopilot can save time and energy sometimes, and it can give you time to think about other things. It can cause trouble, though, when you live most of your life on autopilot, acting out of habit and not being present in the moment. This is especially true when it comes to emotions. Mindfulness can help you take a step back and notice what is really happening in the moment, and help you choose how you react rather than let automatic emotional responses take over. While meditation is a great way to practice mindfulness, DBT has a strong focus on everyday mindfulness, of being aware of the present moment while carrying on with the business of our lives. DBT encourages participating in daily mindfulness exercises to build the muscle of mindfulness.

Goals of Mindfulness

Mindfulness has a number of benefits, both for physical and mental health. Some of these include an increase in happiness and a reduction in emotional suffering, pain, tension, and stress.

The practice of mindfulness helps you increase control of your mind. Sometimes when individuals are struggling with emotion dysregulation, they feel engulfed by their feelings, like there is nothing they can do about it. The practice of mindfulness, over time, allows them to decide what to pay attention to and how long to pay attention to it. In mindfulness we say, "Experience reality as it is," and this means living with your eyes wide open and being present in the moments of your life as they truly are.

The Three States of Mind

Do you remember the previous discussion about dialectics on page 6, and the idea of two opposing ideas being true at the same time? Dialectical thinking comes back into play with the three states of mind. Emotion mind is hot. It is all about feelings and urges. Emotion mind's direct opposite, reasonable mind, is cool. It is about facts and figures and logic. It is about following the protocol. Both emotion and reason have value, but each one on its own can be problematic. In creating a synthesis of these two opposites—taking the best parts of emotion and the best parts of reason and adding a bit of intuition—you get Wise Mind, a state of inner wisdom where we make our best choices.

EMOTION MIND

When Emotion Mind is not balanced by our reasonable mind and Wise Mind, our feelings can be out of control. When in emotion mind, little matters except our immediate feelings and urges. Reason and effectiveness are thrown out the window. The long-term consequences of our actions just don't matter when we are in emotion mind, and it's not the place we want to be when making vital choices that can impact our lives, our jobs, and our relationships.

Don't confuse being highly emotional with being in emotion mind. I really love puppies. I can feel extremely high levels of love and happiness when I see a puppy. If in emotion mind, I would run off with all the puppies and no one would have any puppies because they would all be mine. But despite feeling a strong emotion, in this case, I can still regulate it so that I do not run off with all the puppies. Therefore, I am not in emotion mind, only very emotional.

REASONABLE MIND

Reasonable mind is the logical, rule- and task-oriented part of our psyche. It's essential, of course, to help us be a good citizen or a reliable worker. But when our reasonable mind is not balanced by our emotion mind and Wise Mind, we are ruled solely by facts, rules, and procedures. While reasonable mind can be great for solving math equations and building bridges, it's not always great for our relationships, because reasonable mind can be overly restrained or emotionally distant. For example, someone in reasonable mind might avoid meaningful connection with loved ones in hopes of reducing their reactivity.

WISE MIND

Wise Mind reflects the savvy, prudence, and wisdom that each of us builds over the years, shaped by our daily lives and what we learn from them. It is the ability to balance reason and emotion, but with intuition, foresight, and a broader perspective on "what really matters." We all possess Wise Mind, but some of us have a harder time accessing it than others. It takes a lot of practice to hone Wise Mind.

Wise Mind is the part of each person that can experience truth. This is where we want to be when making important decisions. But how do we get to Wise Mind? By practicing mindfulness.

BASIC MINDFULNESS SKILLS

Mindfulness can be hard to teach, because it is such an experiential activity. But practicing mindfulness is key to learning to practice mindfulness. See what I did there? It's something you *have to do to learn to do*. So be patient with yourself, without judgment, as you learn and practice some mindfulness-based skills.

But first, let's debunk a few myths. Mindfulness is not about having a clear mind or eliminating thoughts altogether. Distractions are going to happen, and your brain is going to think thoughts. That's just the way the brain works. In fact, bringing your attention back to the mindfulness practice helps build the "muscle" of mindfulness. Thanks, distractions! Also, mindfulness is not necessarily about relaxation. Depending on the practice you choose to participate in that day, it can be a nice side effect, but the purpose of mindfulness is not relaxation.

According to Dr. Marsha Linehan, mindfulness includes three "WHAT" skills: observe, describe, and participate; and three "HOW" skills: nonjudgmentally, one-mindfully, and effectively. The WHAT skills are what we do when we practice mindfulness. We can only do them one at a time, and unless we are doing a practice specifically focused on one of the WHAT skills, we flip back and forth between the WHAT skills as we are being mindful. The HOW skills, on the other hand, are applied all at once.

WHAT Skills

The WHAT skills include:

Observe. *You can observe your internal and external world by paying attention to your senses and noticing emotions, thoughts, and body sensations. Think of observing as wordless watching. Have you ever noticed how babies look at the world? They are taking in everything but not applying language. That's our goal with this skill.*

Describe. *With this skill you can put words on the information and experiences you have observed. It's important that you just use factual descriptors, not judgments. Only describe what can be observed. We can describe our inner experience but not the inner experience of another.*

Participate. *With this skill, you enter completely into the present moment. Throw yourself completely into the now. When we participate, we let go of observing and describing and enter fully into the moment.*

PRACTICE OBSERVE

Ideas for practicing the observing skill:

→ Find a small object and look at it closely, paying attention to each detail.

→ Sit by a window. Watch the world go by.

→ Notice the sounds around you and the spaces between the sounds.

→ Listen to a piece of music. Feel the music in your body.

→ When drinking coffee, notice the smell as you bring the cup to your mouth each time you sip.

→ Put a hard candy in your mouth. Notice all the sensations as you eat the candy.

→ Observe your breath as you breathe in and out.

PRACTICE DESCRIBE

Ideas for practicing the describing skill:

→ Find a small object. Describe that object in detail.

→ Describe the behavior of a character in a movie without describing intentions, motives, or outcomes that are not directly shown in the film.

→ Choose a political figure you are not fond of. Describe them without judgment.

→ Find a partner. Choose an object but don't show it to your partner. Ask your partner to draw the object merely from your description.

Ideas for practicing the participating skill:

→ Sing in the car

→ Make art

→ Take an improvisation class

→ Go for a walk, completely immersing yourself in it

→ Dance

→ Build with LEGOs

→ Garden

→ Play a sport

→ Intently participate in a conversation

→ Imagine yourself as connected to the universe

HOW Skills

The HOW skills are:

Nonjudgmentally. *Avoid judging people, places, things, etc., as good nor bad. Let go of "shoulds," and accept something simply as it is. Accept the differences between safe and dangerous, or helpful and harmful, without judging them. But also remember that you will judge because you are human, and humans are built to judge. Note the judgment, let it pass, and move on. And when you do judge, try not to judge your judging.*

One-Mindfully. *Be present in this one moment. And now in this moment. And in this moment. And so on.*

Effectively. *Being effective is about doing what works in a specific situation. It means being skillful to achieve goals. It can mean choosing to be happy (getting what we want or need) over being right. It means playing the game you are in, not the game you wish you were in. We can sabotage our own best interests in our insistence on "making a point" or "being right."*

PRACTICE NONJUDGMENTALLY

Practicing Nonjudgmentally:

→ Notice and count your judgmental thoughts using a golf counter or by making marks on a piece of paper.

→ When you notice yourself having a judgmental thought or making a judgmental statement, replace it with a nonjudgmental thought or statement.

→ Think of something that you dislike. Describe that thing using nonjudgmental words and tone of voice.

→ Practice as much and as often as you can using nonjudgmental descriptions of events, the consequences of events, and your emotional responses to events.

PRACTICE ONE-MINDFULLY

Practicing One-Mindfully:

Put your whole awareness into doing a single activity. This can be washing the dishes, driving the car, walking down the street, or taking a shower. Do this activity slowly, and do not let one movement go by without noticing it. Notice your breathing and your body movements as you do this activity. Nothing else matters other than what you are doing right now. Avoid multitasking.

Practicing Effectively:

→ Notice when you start thinking about arguing who is right or wrong or what is fair or unfair instead of doing what is necessary to get the result that you want.

→ Observe when you begin to get snappy with someone. Ask yourself if this is the most effective behavior in this interaction.

DBT IN ACTION:
PRACTICING MINDFULNESS ACTIVITIES

Christine struggled with mood-dependent behavior. She would find herself giving in to what her emotion mind told her to do, especially when she was depressed. This sometimes resulted in staying in bed, playing video games, and eating little chocolate donuts. After a while she would feel terrible about herself and shame would kick in. Reasonable mind would take over, and she would create an impossible study schedule, put her Xbox in the closet, and go on a restrictive diet. Christine and her therapist discussed the importance of finding a middle path between these two extremes and decided that accessing Wise Mind would help her make more effective choices that struck a better balance. Here are some mindfulness activities Christine used to practice accessing Wise Mind. Try them for yourself.

As you engage in mindful breathing, allow yourself to notice the "pause" after each inhalation and each exhalation. Notice the *stillness* within each pause. Allow yourself to find awareness in the pauses at the top and bottom of each breath. Settle into each pause and find stillness within.

If you find yourself experiencing even the *slightest* sense that you are about to do or are doing something that you will later regret, *notice* this and pause. As you pause, take a slow breath in and ask yourself, "Is this (action, thought, etc.) Wise Mind?" *Listen* for the answer. Allow it to arise naturally within. Pause, breathe, and notice what answer presents itself to you.

As you breathe in, focus on the word "wise," and as you breathe out, focus on the word "mind." Continue until you have the sense that you are in a state of Wise Mind.

HOW TO PRACTICE MINDFULNESS

As you've learned, mindfulness takes practice. And to be successful at emotion regulation, you have to practice it throughout the day, informally. Informal practice is applying mindfulness to whatever you are doing in the moment. It could be anything from taking a few mindful breaths in the middle of the day, to mindfully washing the dishes.

To be able to build the muscle of mindfulness, a more formal practice of engaging in mindful activities is helpful. This, in turn, can help you access Wise Mind. And regular practice can utilize lower-stakes situations, like the impulse to hit the snooze button on the alarm clock, to help with higher-stakes situations, like getting in touch with Wise Mind quickly if self-destructive urges are present.

Here's how to get a daily mindfulness practice in place.

Making Space

When thinking about making space for mindfulness, one has to think about physical space and mental space. Mental space involves allowing yourself to take time for mindfulness. When I first started practicing mindfulness, I found myself feeling irritated and guilty about taking the time. *I'm too busy for this! I should be working! There are other things I need to do!* Mind you, these thoughts were usually about taking the time to do a five-minute mindfulness practice. You may find yourself having thoughts that get in the way of practicing mindfulness. Do yourself a favor and put away those judgments.

As far as physical space goes, we all have varying resources, don't we? Some will be able to have a dedicated room and significant time to allot for mindfulness; others will have to lock themselves in the bathroom for a few minutes of quiet. If you commute, the car (not while driving, of course), bus, or train can be a great place to grab some practice, although not always ideal. A mindful walk can be accomplished when you don't have space to practice mindfulness in a busy household.

Setting a Routine

Making a daily mindfulness practice into a routine (just like exercise) makes it more likely you will participate and form the mindfulness habit. A morning routine can create a more positive and healthier mindset for the rest of the day. A nighttime routine may set you up for restful sleep, if not a relaxing way to end the day. In any case, a daily practice sets the stage for being more mindful in day-to-day life, thereby making it more likely that you will be able to access the mindfulness needed to regulate your emotions and create your life worth living.

KEY TAKEAWAYS

*We've gotten through the first module of DBT skills!
You've seen how mindfulness is practiced and learned
about the three states of mind and how to practice the
WHAT and HOW skills, and you've also gained some
insight into the importance of daily mindfulness practice. As we move forward, it will be helpful to keep in
mind the following:*

→ Building the muscle of mindfulness and being able to
access Wise Mind takes lots of repetition and practice.
Don't expect to be able to trot it out in moments of
intense dysregulation without having done it a bunch
when not dysregulated. Practice now so the muscle
is built for when things hit the fan later. Basketball
players don't hit that free throw in front of thousands of
screaming fans without having practiced free throws
for countless hours on their own.

→ You can do anything mindfully. Just choose your activity. Do that activity. Notice when your attention wanders. Gently bring your attention back.

→ Remember to notice your judgments as judgments,
not facts. This will help you reduce the strong emotions
that tend to be elicited by judgments.

*Our next destination is the crisis survival skill of
Distress Tolerance.*

CHAPTER 5

Understanding How Distress Tolerance Works

In this chapter, we will look at what constitutes a crisis, and how to rate your level of distress in order to help decide what skills to use when. Then, you'll learn all sorts of skills to get through crisis situations without making things worse. You'll also learn about radical acceptance and different ways to accept reality.

DBT FAST FACTS:
SUBJECTIVE UNITS OF DISTRESS SCALE (SUDs)

The subjective units of distress scale (SUDs) is a tool used by clinicians to understand the level of distress someone is experiencing in a given moment. It's subjective because it's from the perspective of the person experiencing it. It's distress because it encompasses the discomfort, pain, and general uncomfortable feeling the person is having.

SUDs is a numbered scale from 0 to 10 or 0 to 100. For our purposes, let's use a 0 to 10 scale. Zero would be no distress. Ten would be the worst distress one could possibly feel.

Being mindful of your SUDs throughout the day can be a great way to get a heads-up on what skills to use when. When your SUDs are lower, change-oriented skills such as those contained in the Emotion Regulation and Interpersonal Regulation modules are probably going to be more successful. The higher the SUDs, the more acceptance-oriented skills are likely to be helpful. When your SUDs is very high, distress tolerance skills are the way to go. Mindfulness skills are all-the-time skills but are also supereffective when your SUDs are high.

WHAT ARE CRISIS SURVIVAL SKILLS?

Crisis survival skills are all about getting through difficult situations without making things worse. Often, when emotions are high, folks will do things that provide relief in the short term but that can really mess things up in the long term. Here's an example:

Sam's partner just started law school and has been less responsive to Sam's calls and texts than usual. Sam, when in

Wise Mind, is aware that law school can be all-consuming, and her partner says her feelings toward Sam remain loving and close. But, sometimes, when Sam doesn't hear from her partner as often as she would like, she feels bereft and alone. Then, emotion mind takes control and Sam texts and calls repeatedly until her partner finally answers. Sam feels short-term relief at getting a response, but after this happens several times, her partner breaks off the relationship because Sam's needs are "just too much right now."

A crisis is a painful, stressful situation that feels like it needs to be resolved or escaped right now. For Sam, the crisis was feeling scared that her partner did not care for her, which was extremely distressing. Giving in to that crisis urge to get reassurance that her partner still cared for her, which provided relief in the short term, was what ultimately caused the end of the relationship. Sam really would have benefited from the use of crisis survival skills to avoid giving in to that crisis urge (repeatedly calling and texting her partner, which ultimately made things much worse).

Crisis survival skills are especially helpful when emotion mind is in charge, when one has strong urges to engage in a target or other destructive behaviors, when one needs to get something done but emotions are getting in the way, or when you need to put a problem on the shelf because there is nothing you can do about it right now.

Distracting Yourself

One technique for getting through a crisis without making things worse is distracting yourself from the problem at hand and putting your attention on something else. No, it is not solving the problem, but when the problem can't be solved right now, this technique will keep you from making things worse. The idea here is that you commit fully to engaging in the skill instead of whatever behavior you are tempted to engage in. Dr. Linehan calls this skill Wise Mind ACCEPTS.

A: Activities. *Throw yourself completely into distracting activities: read, watch TV, clean house, go for a walk.*

C: Contributing. *Help someone else: volunteer, make someone a gift, send someone an encouraging note or text. This has the benefit of not only distracting you but also making you feel good about yourself.*

C: Comparisons. *There are two different ways to practice this skill: One way is to compare your situation to those who are less fortunate than you. This can create an attitude of gratitude for some folks—a reminder to feel grateful for all they have. For others, it can create a feeling of shame or guilt for feeling overwhelmed by "first-world problems." For those folks, it can be helpful to compare how skillfully you are handling this situation now compared to a time in the past.*

E: Emotions. *Do something that creates a different emotion than the one you are currently feeling. If sad, watch a funny television show; if anxious, listen to soothing music.*

P: Pushing away. *Either physically distance yourself from the problem or block it from your mind. For instance, build an imaginary wall between you and the coworker who hums incessantly, or place concerns that nothing can be done about in a box and put them away in a drawer.*

T: Thoughts. *Distract yourself by focusing on other thoughts: saying the alphabet backward, remembering the words to old sitcom theme songs, doing crosswords or sudoku—anything that keeps your mind busy.*

S: Sensations. *You can also use strong physical sensations to distract from strong emotions: hold a piece of ice in your hand or your mouth, take a hot or cold shower, smell an intense scent, or taste something strongly flavored.*

Soothing Yourself

Using the five senses as a launching point, focus mindfully on soothing activities when your SUDs are high. This allows you to focus on something other than what is causing you to feel strong emotions and gives you the chance to soothe yourself at the same time.

Here are some ideas:

Sight. *Sit and watch a sunset or visit nature. People-watch or look at beautiful pictures in a book.*

Smell. *Enjoy scented candles, essential oils, or freshly cut grass, or bake some bread.*

Hearing. *Focus intently on the birds chirping outside, play soothing music, or focus on the sounds of water.*

Taste. *Brew a cup of tea, roll a mint around in your mouth, or eat one thing really mindfully.*

Touch. *Climb into comfy jammies, take a bubble bath, give yourself a hug, or stroke your dog or cat (they will concur that this is a great idea).*

USING CRISIS SURVIVAL SKILLS TO CURB IMPULSIVE BEHAVIORS

When emotions are high, impulsive behavior can follow. When emotion mind takes control, people often feel that they have no other choice than to engage in emotion-mind urges. While it can feel this way, being more mindful, learning more about internal and external triggers, and regularly practicing skills all lead to being able to resist these urges. One very important thing to remember is that often, being skillful requires using more than one skill. You've already learned two sets of crisis survival skills: Wise Mind ACCEPTS and self-soothing. Sometimes, having other skills to use prior to or in addition to using those skills can be helpful. Many of the skills in this section can be helpful to use when your SUDs are very high. Take particular note of the STOP skill and the TIPP skills as things to do when you feel high levels of emotion to prepare to use other crisis survival skills. Also, doing pros and cons prior to being in crisis can be very helpful.

Using the STOP Method

When emotion mind is in charge, people often act impulsively. Dr. Linehan recommends the STOP skill for putting some space between a trigger and your response. This skill can help you take a minute and give yourself space to get to Wise Mind in order to avoid giving in to crisis urges.

STOP

Seriously, stop! Don't move! Freeze for a moment before the urge to react takes over.

TAKE A STEP BACK

Remove yourself either physically or mentally. Take a few deep breaths. Do not let your urge to react take over.

OBSERVE

Just the facts, please. Observe and describe what is really happening. No judgments, assumptions, or interpretations.

PROCEED MINDFULLY

Ask your Wise Mind what the best response might be. What outcome will you feel best about tomorrow or next week? Proceeding mindfully might be going to another crisis survival skill like ACCEPTS, self-soothing, IMPROVE (page 73), or using other skills in other chapters in this book.

Using Pros and Cons

We do the pros and cons of engaging in certain behaviors all the time. We decide whether or not to push the snooze button again, drink another cup of coffee, or watch one more episode of that show on Netflix based on the pros and cons of doing so. We just don't tend to write out a list.

A pros and cons list is intended to be done in advance of a triggering situation, when you are in Wise Mind. It's intended to be a tip sheet from your Wise Mind on the preferred response to a triggering situation. In the midst of an emotion-mind tsunami, sometimes it can be hard to remember why it's so important not to give in to emotion-mind urges. Listing out the pros and cons in advance and reviewing them multiple times prior to a trigger occurring, and again during a triggering situation, can be very helpful in resisting crisis urges.

ARTICULATING THE BEHAVIOR

In this type of pros and cons list, you will be listing the pros and cons for acting on crisis urges and the pros and cons of resisting crisis urges. So, it's a bit more involved than a typical pros and cons list.

Here is an example for us to practice on: A customer at the store you work at has made loud, negative comments about you in front of your coworkers and other customers. You want to make the customer stop doing this. Your action urge is to tell the customer off and then throw him out of the store. The problem? Your boss is of the belief that you should laugh off the customer's comments, and she has made it clear that the customer is welcome in the store. If you engage in your action urge you will be fired. You are working on your résumé, but you can't go without a paycheck, even for a short time.

	PROS	CONS
Acting on crisis urges, e.g., yelling at customer, kicking him out of store	It would feel so good to kick him out of the store and tell him what a jerk he is! He wouldn't get away with his bad behavior! Let him be publicly shamed for once!	No job = no money Just one more thing my family can use to say that I have anger management issues. I committed to using DBT skills, and giving in to my urges wouldn't be skillful.
Resisting crisis urges, e.g., not yelling at customer, and instead being civil, ignoring negative comments	I would feel very skillful. Yay adulting! My boss would probably give me a good reference for my job search. My family wouldn't be able to hold it over me that I got fired for going off on someone. I would have money coming in while I look for a new job.	I wouldn't get to tell the jerk where to go. I would feel like I wasn't standing up for myself.

Now that the list is made, we can go through and see whether giving in to the crisis urges of kicking that dude out of the store and losing the job are worth it. In this case, it seems that long-term goals of maintaining self-respect (being skillful) and keeping that money coming in while looking for a new job win out over the short-term goal of telling that customer where to get off.

TIPP your Body Chemistry

When your SUDs are running high, the physiological reactions can feel overwhelmingly strong. Fortunately, there are ways to lower the intensity of the emotion to release its grip on your body. This is where TIPP skills come in. TIPP skills are intended to tip your body chemistry to reduce sympathetic nervous system activity and increase parasympathetic nervous system activity. Our autonomic nervous system has two responses: 1) the sympathetic nervous system, which is associated with the fight-flight-freeze response, and 2) the parasympathetic nervous system, associated with the "rest and digest" response. Using one of the following skills in a crisis can reduce physiological and emotional arousal quickly and get you into a place where you can then use other coping skills.

TEMPERATURE

A temperature change can induce the "mammalian dive reflex" (think of an animal holding its breath underwater). This reflex can put the parasympathetic nervous system into operation, thereby reducing the physiological arousal that often accompanies intense emotions. (See the Resources section on page 142 for a video explaining the science behind this.) Before you try this technique, however, check with your medical provider, especially if you have cardiac problems, suffer from an eating disorder (including anorexia or bulimia), or deal with other medical issues (especially those related to your heart). Cleared for takeoff? To kick off the dive reflex, hold your breath and immerse your face in cold water (but not colder than 50°F) for 30 to 60 seconds. You can get the same effect by filling a zip-top bag with ice cubes or cold water, wrapping it in a damp paper towel, and holding it over your eyes and cheeks. Even a cold washcloth on your face may do the trick. If using the bag or washcloth, hold your breath to intensify the effect.

INTENSE EXERCISE

Engaging in intense cardio/aerobic exercise followed by a cooldown can de-escalate intense emotions, like fear or anger, that prime your body to run or attack. Ideally, try to exercise for twenty minutes or more, hitting 70 percent of your maximum heart rate. After the exercise, pay attention as you cool down and note what it feels like. As you cool down from intense exercise, the body is reregulating itself to a calmer state.

PACED BREATHING

Paced breathing is a great way to get the parasympathetic nervous system online when faced with a triggering situation. Inhaling activates the sympathetic nervous system. It prepares us for action. Exhaling activates the parasympathetic nervous system, which calms us down. The trick here is to spend more time exhaling than inhaling so your body gets to slow down and calm down.

Here's the basic technique: 1. Inhale for a count of two to four seconds. 2. Exhale for a count of four to six seconds. 3. Continue for as long as desired. Find the combination that works for you, making sure to exhale longer than you inhale.

Here are some things to keep in mind as you go:

→ Breathe in slowly through your nose, letting your chest and lower belly expand with each inhalation.

→ Breathe out slowly through your mouth. For maximum calming effects, try to slow your breathing down to five or six breath cycles per minute.

This breathing exercise works even better when you practice in advance of triggering situations, because you will have trained yourself to be able to activate the relaxation response more readily.

PAIRED MUSCLE RELAXATION

To practice paired muscle relaxation, you tense muscle groups while you breathe in and then relax the muscles as you breathe out. You'll want to notice the sensations of tension and relaxation as you practice. For example, you might clench your fists, forearms, and upper arms as you breathe in, noticing the tension, and then relax those muscles as you exhale, noticing the muscles letting go. Some folks practice paired muscle relaxation by saying the word "relax" in their minds while they exhale, as a kind of mantra. If you do this consistently, your mind and body can begin to associate the word "relax" with an easing of tension, and it might be possible to say this word and elicit a relaxation response, even without engaging in the full exercise.

By IMPROVE-ing the Moment

The "improve the moment" skill is comprised of a menu of options you can use to shift your focus by making your negative experience a more positive one. So, if you are in a crisis and there's nothing you can do to solve the problem, at least you can try to make your current experience a little bit better. Here are some options, which make up the acronym IMPROVE:

IMAGERY

Imagery can be used in many ways. You can focus on the sights around you. You can imagine yourself in a peaceful, soothing place. You can imagine stress and painful emotions flowing out of you. You can even picture yourself coping extraordinarily well with whatever situation you find yourself in.

MEANING

Find meaning in the painful situation you face. Focus on whatever positives you can find in your current scenario. How can what you learn from this situation be used to help others?

PRAYER

Prayer means different things to different people. You might view prayer as accessing Wise Mind or turning things over to something bigger than yourself. Perhaps you believe in a higher power. However you tap this skill, ask for the strength to bear the situation, not for the situation to magically disappear.

RELAXATION

There are so many things that can bring a bit of relaxation to a difficult situation. Perhaps a few deep breaths? A walk, some yoga, or a nice bath? Relaxing activities can bring you to a better place to deal with current challenges, and at least they can't make things worse.

ONE THING IN THE MOMENT

Bring a mindful focus to whatever you are doing in the moment. Notice when your mind starts to get caught up in painful thoughts about the past or fears for the future. Instead, focus intently on the task you currently need to perform. Are you washing the dishes? Notice everything about the task: the bubbles, the warmth of the water, the sound of the sponge, etc.

VACATION

This doesn't mean pack your bags and run away to Bermuda! It means planning a brief respite from your current challenges. That means making a plan to return to real life, too. If you are going to take a one-hour breather from life, make sure you set a timer and commit to returning when the timer goes off. Now, go take a break!

ENCOURAGEMENT

Sometimes, we all need some cheerleading. We can tell ourselves, "This is hard, but I can do it," "I am doing the best I can," "Go Team Me!" or "This, too, shall pass." The important part is to talk to yourself the same way you would talk to someone you love.

DBT IN ACTION: CRISIS SURVIVAL KITS

Travis was new to DBT, and things were going well. But, boy, it seemed like his SUDs went from 0 to 10 out of nowhere, and getting those crisis survival skills going before he gave in to crisis urges felt really hard.

Travis and his therapist decided that increasing his mindfulness throughout the day and rating his SUDs often would help him catch variations in his emotional level so that he could intervene with skills before his SUDs got too high.

Travis played a lot of sports throughout his life and understood the value of doing drills of basic skills so that there would be muscle memory when needed in crucial moments. Travis committed to practicing paced breathing, paired muscle relaxation, and STOP several times throughout the day so they would be easier to access when he needed them.

Travis also set up a few crisis survival kits in his home, car, and office, with pros and cons lists for his crisis urges, as well as distracting activities, a few self-soothing objects, and some things to improve the moment. He also put some ice packs in his fridge so that he could use the TIPP temperature skill. He even got some of those instant emergency ice packs to keep in his car in case he needs to tip his body chemistry on the road.

HOW TO PRACTICE
RADICAL ACCEPTANCE

Not everything in life is fair or works out how we want it to. Sometimes this is small stuff like being stuck in traffic, but sometimes it's the big stuff like losing someone we love or having been abused during childhood. In any case, these things are reality. They happened and we can't make them unhappen.

People often say, "I cannot stand it," "This shouldn't have happened," or "He shouldn't have done that," when something that we find painful or don't like happens. It's as if we believe we can prevent something from being true by refusing to accept reality. Let's say you experienced terrible hurt. Refusing to accept it won't make it unhappen. Focusing on how it should have been different won't make it unhappen, either. Accepting doesn't mean you have to like or approve of what happened. You do not have to accept anything other than the facts of the situation, and you only have to accept right now. For example, you only have to accept that the person you like didn't text you back, not that you are doomed to a life of loneliness and despair.

Fighting reality is exhausting, and it's pretty darn pointless. Rejecting what has already happened does not change reality, AND it also adds other negative emotions to the pain we already feel. The equation looks something like this: Reality + acceptance of reality = pain. However, reality + nonacceptance of reality = pain and suffering. Pain is hard enough, but adding suffering to the mix makes it feel even worse.

Radical acceptance is a way to turn unnecessary suffering into ordinary pain. You may also notice a sense of sadness as you grieve what could have been. But ultimately, acceptance can bring a sense of calm, centeredness, and peace.

Turning the Mind

Radical acceptance isn't a skill that you do once about a specific situation and then you mark it off the list. Have you ever lost your wallet? You check everywhere. And then, eventually, painfully, you try to accept that your wallet is gone. But do you really accept it? No! You go back and check again. Why? Because acceptance is hard! So, you try accepting it for a bit and then go back to looking for your wallet. And it's even harder when it's a bigger issue. At first you're accepting, then suddenly you find you're not. This is where turning the mind comes into play. Think about being at a fork in the road. Your choice is to take the road to acceptance or the road to nonacceptance. Which way do you turn? Turn your mind toward acceptance, of course!

NOTICE AND COMMIT

But how is this done? Step 1: Notice that you aren't accepting. Step 2: Commit. Step 3: Turn the mind toward acceptance. Do this over and over, whenever you notice you are not accepting reality.

Willingness vs. Willfulness

What if you're still having trouble accepting reality? Welcome to being human. It happens to us all. It can be difficult to accept the cards life deals out to us, but getting upset or threatening to quit the game doesn't change the cards you get. In DBT we call this act of refusing to accept the cards you are dealt "willfulness." Playing the cards you get, even when you don't like them, is "willingness." Willingness is listening to Wise Mind and doing what is needed in each specific situation. Willfulness is giving up, wanting to be in control of every situation, demanding that things change immediately. Willingness is vital to acceptance. Willfulness gets in the way of acceptance. Being willing to accept something does not mean you like or approve of the situation. And it is often the first step to making changes. Let's say you want to make changes to society. Just standing there and demanding them simply doesn't work. Accepting that one might need to work incrementally to change a broken society might result in change over the long term.

Willing Hands and Half-Smile

Still having trouble accepting reality? Your body can help. Virtually all of us have seen a statue of the Buddha. He looks pretty relaxed, right? That's partly because of two things: his sweet, soothing facial expression and his open, upward-facing hands. With this image of the Buddha in mind, try practicing the willing hands and half-smile. The half-smile is a way of reflecting to yourself that you accept reality by letting go with your body. The brain and the facial muscles are closest to each other and communicate very quickly. Change that expression, and you just might feel more accepting. Here's how to half-smile: Relax your face, neck, and shoulder muscles. Then, just slightly tilt up the sides of your lips in a gentle half-smile. It won't be noticeable to anyone but you. It tends to register to others as an expression of neutral interest. No one has to see you smile. You are not smiling at anyone else. You are smiling at your brain. "Hey, brain, all is well. We're good." "Willing hands" is a way of demonstrating that you accept reality by letting go with your body. Open your hands, palms up and fingers relaxed. It is a very open and accepting posture.

KEY TAKEAWAYS

We've covered a lot of distance in this chapter. You've learned how to get through bad situations without making things worse, and you've learned how accepting pain can reduce suffering. As we move forward, it will be helpful to keep in mind:

→ Keep an eye on your subjective units of distress scale (SUDs). By tuning mindfully into your sources of distress, you can gain helpful clues about what skills to use when. Crisis survival skills are most useful when your SUDs are high. Mindfulness skills are all-the-time skills but are especially useful when your SUDs are high. Emotion regulation and interpersonal effectiveness skills are generally more effective when your SUDs are lower.

→ Assemble crisis survival kits for your home, office, car, etc., with go-to skills reminders, pros and cons lists, distracting activities, self-soothing items, and improve-the-moment objects to make it easier to be skillful in the moment.

→ Practice radical acceptance as often as you can. At any moment, throw your body, mind, and soul into accepting reality as it is right now. It is not easy, but it is the road to peace and freedom.

CHAPTER 6

Understanding How Emotion Regulation Works

In this chapter, we are going to look at what emotions do for us and learn more about their purpose and function. You'll learn how to reduce vulnerability to emotions by taking care of your mind and body. You'll also learn how to change emotions when they don't fit the facts of the situation or aren't effective to act upon. And finally, we'll explore the balance between self-sufficiency with skills use and reaching out to others for assistance.

DBT FAST FACTS:
THE PLEASANT EVENTS LIST

Positive events are important for emotional health.
Dr. Marsha Linehan recommends that we each participate
in at least one pleasant event daily, and more, if possible, to
build resilience against negative emotions. It is important to
be mindful and participate fully in the activity, not just plop
yourself in front of the television for a mind-numbing Netflix
binge. A pleasant activity someone else enjoys might be
boring or distasteful to you, so feel free to make your own list.

→ go for a walk

→ talk to a friend

→ ride a bike

→ listen to music

→ watch a movie

→ go to
the beach

→ exercise

→ read a book

→ play an
instrument

→ go swimming

→ spend time
with your pet

→ get a coffee

→ organize your
room or home

→ do a puzzle

→ go for a hike

→ save money

→ plan a trip

→ dance

→ go out
for a meal

→ watch sports

→ think positive
things about
the future

→ make up songs
about your cat

→ make
to-do lists

→ take photos

→ hug someone

→ go thrifting

→ bake a cake

THE THREE FUNCTIONS
OF EMOTIONS

When folks have struggled with emotion dysregulation, they sometimes become a little emotionally phobic, or a bit scared of experiencing emotions, because of the trouble that emotions have caused for them. Others express concerns that learning to regulate emotions will turn them into unfeeling, overregulated robots. The goal of regulating emotions is not to get rid of emotions. The truth is that emotions have purpose. Fear helps us run from danger. Anger helps us fight to protect ourselves. Love makes us search for those who are lost. Shame can keep us from acting in ways that may cause us to be rejected by our tribe. Guilt helps us make repairs when we have violated our values.

Communicating Information to Yourself

Emotions are little voices inside us, our instincts, giving us our sense about ourselves, situations, or other people. Treating feelings as facts, however, can be problematic. For example, if I had no information about someone that I had just met other than the feeling that they were trustworthy, I wouldn't want to treat this feeling as a fact and sign over all of my worldly goods to them.

Communicating and Influencing Others

Our emotions communicate messages and influence others. Facial expressions communicate faster than words. When a loved one sees us with a sad facial expression, it can lead them to reach out to comfort us. We don't necessarily have to say a word.

Emotional expressions associated with warmth and friend-liness (like smiling, using a warm tone of voice, open body posture) can draw others closer to us. But what if our verbal and nonverbal expressions of emotion don't match? Research published in the *Quarterly Journal of Experimental Psychology* indicates that people will almost always trust nonverbal expressions over verbal expressions of emotion. Remember that the next time you tell someone you care about that nothing's wrong when they know you're mad as hell.

Motivating Action

Emotions prepare us for action. I grew up in Southern California during a time when there was a lot of earthquake activity. Even now, when I feel the ground shake, I feel fear and start to activate to find a safe place for myself and whoever I'm with. The feeling of fear is helpful; it saves time. I don't have to think everything through. Shaking and fear are connected in my brain to mean earthquake. That's great when it's actually an earthquake. The emotion is justified by the facts of the situation, and my action of looking for a safe place works for the facts. But what if I stay afraid once I realize it was just a truck driving by? Later in this chapter we'll talk about using exercises called "check the facts" and "opposite action" when our reactions don't serve our goals in a particular situation.

HOW TO DECREASE EMOTIONAL VULNERABILITY

Have you ever noticed that when you are taking care of your body and mind, you are less likely to be rocked by events that bring about negative emotions and more able to brush things off or let things go? That's what this set of skills is all about. The skills in this section help folks build lives that make them less vulnerable to negative emotions, to help build up a bit more of a thicker emotional skin by being proactive about taking care of oneself in advance of difficult events. You know when people talk about self-care and everybody thinks it's all about manicures, bubble baths, and face masks? The ABC PLEASE skills are about real self-care. This is especially important for folks who are facing a lot of difficulties in life and need to be especially effective in order to reach their goals.

Using ABC

The ABC part of ABC PLEASE is primarily about taking care of your mind by preparing in advance for difficult times and shoring up your resources now. The A stands for accumulating positive emotions, both in the short and the long term. The B is for building mastery, i.e., doing things that make you feel like you can do hard things. And C is for coping ahead, for practicing in advance for difficult emotional situations so you feel prepared and able to manage them.

ACCUMULATING POSITIVES

Big surprise, but people who experience more pleasant events tend to have fewer negative emotions. Likewise, the absence of positive experiences tends to lead to negative emotions. So, it is super important for your mental health to do things that are pleasant. These can be small events like mindfully eating a piece of chocolate. The important part is to fully engage in the experience and let go of worries while you participate.

We also need to accumulate long-term, positive events, such as achieving goals that are important to us or building lasting relationships. One way to do this is to identify our values, choose goals based on those values, and then identify action steps we can take now to reach those goals over time.

BUILDING MASTERY

Feeling competent and accomplished helps you feel better. Doing activities that make us feel confident and accomplished, even small tasks, fall under the "building mastery" skill.

Building mastery is all about consciously choosing to do at least one thing each day, big or small, to feel accomplished and productive.

→ Plan for success, not failure. Choose something that's a challenge but isn't impossible. For example, if you have never run as exercise before, don't plan to run three miles your first day.

→ Gradually increase the difficulty over time. Small progress is still progress!

→ Look for a challenge. If the thing you try today is too easy, try something harder tomorrow!

COPING AHEAD

Often, we have one of two responses in advance of a stress-provoking situation. One is that we try to avoid thinking about the situation at all. The other is that we ruminate about all the horrible things that could happen in that particular situation. The "cope-ahead" skill involves rehearsing ahead of time so that you are prepared to cope skillfully with emotional situations.

1. Describe the situation that is likely to prompt uncomfortable emotions. Check the facts. Be specific in describing the situation. Name the emotions and actions likely to interfere with using your skills.

2. Decide what skills you want to use in the situation. Be very specific. Write out in detail how you will cope with the situation and with your emotions and action urges.

3. Imagine the situation in your mind as vividly as possible. Imagine yourself in the situation now, not watching the situation.

4. Rehearse in your mind exactly what you can do to cope effectively. Rehearse your actions, your thoughts, what you say, and how to say it. Rehearse coping effectively with new problems that come up. Rehearse coping effectively with the worst-case scenario.

5. Take some time to practice relaxation after you have practiced coping ahead.

6. Put that plan into action when the time comes. You've got this!

Using PLEASE

PLEASE is a set of skills all about taking care of your body in order to take care of your mind and reduce your vulnerability to negative emotions. Ever been hangry? Being hungry makes us more vulnerable to the negative emotion of anger.

PL: *Treat **P**hysical i**L**lness. See a doctor when needed and take your prescribed medications.*

E: *Balance your **E**ating. Eat regularly throughout the day, and refrain from eating too much or too little for your needs.*

A: ***A**void mood-altering substances. Keep away from alcohol (or use with moderation), and do not take nonprescribed drugs.*

S: *Balance your **S**leep. Get enough sleep and stick to a consistent sleep schedule.*

E: *Get plenty of **E**xercise. Even if you are not running marathons, do some sort of physical movement every day.*

HOW TO CHANGE EMOTIONAL RESPONSES

Often, people react immediately and automatically to a situation or someone else's behavior, especially if they are emotionally sensitive. The result: an emotional response. The first step is for you to determine whether that emotion is justified or unjustified. It's not about judging whether your emotion is right or wrong, but more about whether the emotion is helpful, unhelpful, or causing you suffering. In DBT, determining whether an emotion is justified or unjustified involves checking the facts of the situation to determine whether the emotion and/or its duration or intensity fits the facts of the situation.

Justified Emotion: Your emotion, along with its duration and its intensity, fits the facts of a situation. For example: being mildly (intensity) annoyed (emotion) for two minutes (duration) when you find out your lunch delivery will be fifteen minutes late.

Unjustified Emotion: Your emotion either doesn't fit the facts of the situation or its intensity or duration (or a combination of any or all three) does not fit the facts of the situation. For example: feeling overwhelming (intensity) shame (emotion) for days (duration) after your boss points out a minor mistake you made in front of a coworker. In this case, anyone might feel a little shame for a brief period of time, but what makes this emotion unjustified is the overwhelming level of intensity and the duration of days.

Practicing Check the Facts

To refocus an emotional response, you can ask yourself these questions to check whether that response is justified by the situation. You may find your emotion or its intensity changing as you answer.

1. What is the emotion I feel that I want to change?

2. Describe the situation that brought about this emotion using facts only. No judgments!

3. What are your assumptions and interpretations about the situation? Would someone completely impartial agree with your interpretations?

4. Are you assuming a threat to your life, your way of life, or your livelihood? What is that threat? How likely is it really to occur? What else could happen?

5. Is this a catastrophe? If it is (when you really think about it, it almost never is), imagine the catastrophe occurring, and you coping well with it.

6. Ask Wise Mind: Does my emotion or its intensity fit the facts now that I've looked at them?

You may find that checking the facts leads to a change in your emotion, or you may find the intensity of your emotion decreasing. If not, "opposite action" is next on the list.

Practicing Opposite Action

Opposite action is the skill to use when you feel an emotion and acting on the accompanying action urge would be ineffective.

Emotions have associated action urges. When angry, many people feel an urge to attack, verbally or physically; when sad, to withdraw or isolate; when ashamed, to hide or avoid; when in love, to be close to that person; and when afraid, to run or avoid.

For example, how about feeling a high level of anxiety that leads to an urge to avoid elevators, but the interview for your dream job is on the 63rd floor! First of all, the emotion is unjustified by the facts of the situation. You are super unlikely to die on that elevator. It is also unjustified because it is ineffective for your goals. You WANT that job, and you suspect that you are the most qualified candidate. Rather than give in to the urge to avoid that elevator, do the opposite action: get on that elevator and ace the interview!

Remember in chapter 5 when we talked about willingness (page 78)? Opposite action requires a lot of willingness. But the results are quite powerful. Opposite action helps us understand that our emotions are not the boss of us, and that we can be in charge. Here's how:

IDENTIFY AND NAME YOUR EMOTION

Here are some emotions to pick from, or you can use an emotion name of your own.

→ Fear	→ Shame	→ Envy
→ Anger	→ Happiness	→ Love
→ Sadness	→ Jealousy	→ Guilt

You may be feeling more than one emotion. How intense is the emotion or emotions you are feeling? Rate the intensity from 0 to 100.

CHECK YOUR FACTS

Does your emotion fit the facts? Does the duration of the emotion fit the facts? Does the intensity? For example, being annoyed with your partner for not unloading the dishwasher is justified; being murderous with rage is not.

DETERMINE YOUR ACTION URGE

What do you feel like doing? What are your urges? What do you want to say? What does emotion mind want you to do?

CONNECT WITH WISE MIND

Check in with Wise Mind. "What are the consequences of acting on this urge? Is it going to create problems down the road or make the situation worse?" If yes, then definitely act opposite to your action urges.

IDENTIFY WAYS TO ACT IN OPPOSITION TO YOUR EMOTIONS

When you have determined that acting opposite to your action urge is in your best interest, then it is time to figure out how to act opposite ALL THE WAY. No halfsies here. For our example of getting on the elevator, that means eyes open, shoulders back and relaxed, with a confident body posture. Breathing in and out, perhaps doing paced breathing like you learned in chapter 5 (page 72). Fully being present while riding the elevator. No cringing in the corner with eyes closed, holding your breath. Opposite action works when you are open and willing. Over time, you'll be riding elevators like a champ.

How about that high level of anger at your partner about the dishwasher? The action urges for anger, including yelling, the silent treatment, and sarcasm, aren't likely to make the situation better and will probably start a big fight. One way to do the opposite action for anger urges ALL THE WAY in this situation might be to feel compassion for your partner and try to see the situation from their point of view. Your body is a big help in doing the opposite action, too. Try willing hands and half-smile from chapter 5 (page 79), relax the muscles of your shoulders, chest, and stomach, and do some paced breathing, or even go for a run. And don't worry, the next chapter focuses on interpersonal effectiveness strategies that make it more likely that others will do what you want them to do, like unload the dishwasher.

DBT IN ACTION: BEING MINDFUL OF YOUR SUDs

Amanda loved her family, but big family events were hard. Amanda and her partner really wanted children and were doing what their fertility specialist said to do, but it was distressing to them both when yet another month passed with no good news. It seemed like extended family members were always announcing a pregnancy or having a baby shower. Amanda was starting to dread going to family events. She needed to figure out how to cope, or she would be even more isolated and alone than she already felt. She and her therapist worked on a cope-ahead plan for family events.

Amanda told her therapist that she often felt sadness and shame when she heard a family member announce a pregnancy, and her action urge was often to cry and leave the situation. Amanda also said she felt the urge to tell her partner to leave her and find a woman with better fertility, which often led to arguments between them. Amanda and her therapist decided that being especially mindful of her SUDs prior to and throughout the family event would be important. Amanda decided to practice paced breathing and willing hands and half-smile on the way to the next family event, and every time she saw a baby or pregnant person at the event. She felt this would make her less vulnerable to strong emotion in case someone did announce a pregnancy. She also decided to practice opposite action. If she felt the urge to tell her partner to find a more fertile woman, she would instead give her partner a hug and tell them she loved them.

Amanda's therapist encouraged her to vividly imagine herself using these skills effectively and dealing with the worst-case scenarios she could imagine by using these skills. By practicing this, she felt much more confident about her ability to skillfully navigate her next family event.

HOW TO BE YOUR OWN EMOTIONAL SUPPORT

Struggling with emotion dysregulation can be quite difficult, and knowing when to reach out for help and when to practice self-reliance is often a difficult line to walk. Loved ones and therapists are there to help, and at the same time, learning to self-soothe and use skills leads to building mastery and competence for folks who are prone to dysregulation. Finding that middle path between reaching out to others and being one's own emotional support is key for people learning to regulate their emotions in a healthy way. Supporting people in being their own emotional support systems can sometimes be the most loving thing family members and therapists can do. The more DBT skills are practiced, the more they come naturally, and the more confident people become in their ability to manage difficult emotions. If you struggle with regulation, use skills as often as possible prior to reaching out for help. You'll thank yourself as you become more effective at emotion regulation. Keep the following in mind:

Be Kind to Yourself

People who find that they benefit from DBT have often spent years flooding themselves with self-loathing and judgmental thoughts. And, as we've discussed earlier, they are often emotionally sensitive, which is like being naked in a sandpaper world. The world can just be really overstimulating, and even the good stuff can feel like too much sometimes. It's okay to make extra time for yourself and treat yourself with care. Making self-care a priority can often make a big difference between being effective in day-to-day skills use and blowing skills off and just letting mood-dependent behavior happen. Adhering to the PLEASE skill is important for people who are emotionally sensitive.

And being willing to talk back to those self-loathing thoughts, treating them as just white noise, and encouraging yourself in your efforts, is an important part of your success.

Reappraise Your Thoughts and Feelings

A big part of DBT is staying in touch with reality through mindfulness and recognizing when thoughts and feelings are leading you astray. Simply having a thought doesn't make it true, and simply having an urge doesn't mean you have to act on it. Learning to recognize your own patterns of unhelpful thoughts, feelings, and reactions in different situations can be helpful in adopting a set of skills to fall back on. Having compassion for yourself and not judging yourself for these patterns also helps reduce the level of your reactions. Beating yourself up for needing to use skills or for forgetting to use skills is totally anti-DBT! If you fall off the DBT wagon, don't waste time yelling at yourself. Accept that you fell off and hop back on.

KEY TAKEAWAYS

We've traveled through the module of Emotion Regulation. You've learned the functions of emotions and how to reduce vulnerability to negative emotions. You've seen how checking the facts and using opposite action can change your emotions. As we move forward, it will be helpful to keep in mind:

→ Do not underplay the importance of mindfully participating in pleasant events. Everyone needs positive events in their lives to be happy—especially individuals who are struggling. Use opposite action to engage in pleasant events when sadness or other negative emotions say "no!"

→ Please use PLEASE. The PLEASE skill is key in reducing vulnerability to negative emotions. When we are not sleeping well, eating right, are sick, or are taking drugs that aren't prescribed to us, it makes us prone to all kinds of negative emotions. Taking care of our bodies also builds mastery.

→ When experiencing an emotion that does not fit the facts of the situation or is too intense or is lasting too long, opposite action can help. Figure out your action urge and do the opposite until your emotion changes. Every day can be opposite day!

CHAPTER 7

Understanding How Interpersonal Effectiveness Works

In this chapter we'll take a look at what gets in the way of being interpersonally effective. After that, you'll learn how to balance your emphasis in your communications. You'll see how the DEAR MAN skill can help you get what you want in an interaction. You'll discover how to improve your relationships with validation and the GIVE skill. Finally, you'll learn how to maintain your self-respect using the FAST skill.

DBT FAST FACTS:
OBSERVE, DESCRIBE, PARTICIPATE

Being mindful in our interactions with others makes our relationships stronger and last longer. Look to the WHAT skills of mindfulness (observe, describe, and participate) to guide you in relational mindfulness:

Observe

→ Be curious and interested: pay attention.

→ Be open to change: people change their beliefs, thoughts, desires, and competencies.

→ Drop the overfocus on self.

→ Stay in the here and now: listen to others in real time rather than planning what you will say next.

Describe

→ Avoid judgments and assumptions: Don't assume you know why someone is acting a specific way. When in doubt, check it out.

→ Give others the benefit of the doubt and avoid assuming ill intent (unless Wise Mind concurs): Just because something someone did made you angry doesn't mean they meant to make you angry. Again, when in doubt, check it out.

Participate

→ Jump into the interaction: don't stand on the edge of the conversation—get into it.

→ Fully participate in groups: Let go of focus on yourself and become one with the group activity or conversation.

WHAT IS INTERPERSONAL EFFECTIVENESS?

Interpersonal effectiveness is all about asking for what you want and saying no while maintaining your relationships and your self-respect. These skills help with figuring out what you want and getting others to take your opinions seriously, as well as building and strengthening relationships. They also help us tend to our relationships and deal with conflicts and problems as they arise, rather than letting resentments build up until relationships blow up or break down. They are among the most important and effective skills in the DBT arsenal. But some people who learn these skills write them off and say they don't work. Why? They try them once or twice and don't get what they want. These skills aren't guaranteed to make others automatically pony up with the goods, or automatically stop doing stuff we find annoying. Sometimes people just want to do what they want to do. Some don't know DBT or don't want to play by the rules of DBT. There are lots of obstacles to interpersonal effectiveness, both for those who know DBT skills and those who don't. We'll go over those in a bit more detail in a minute.

Please learn these skills and practice them frequently. While you will not always get what you want, you will benefit no matter what.

Obstacles to Interpersonal Effectiveness

Relationships are tough. Everyone struggles with communicating in relationships. Add emotion dysregulation to the mix, and it gets even tougher. Here we'll go over factors that can interfere with being interpersonally effective.

LACKING SKILLS

When you lack skills in interpersonal situations, it means you don't know what to do. It may mean you don't know what to say or don't know how to act. Sometimes we just don't have the opportunity to learn from role models how to manage social situations, or we don't get the chance to practice certain social behaviors. We'll address this barrier later in the chapter. You'll learn skills that will help you build your effectiveness when interacting with others.

NOT KNOWING WHAT YOU WANT

Maybe you know what to say, what to do, or how to act. But maybe you don't know what it is that you really want. Not being clear about what you want gets confusing when you are trying to communicate. You may also have trouble knowing how to balance your needs with the needs of others, and when it's okay to ask for your needs to be met and when it's okay to say no to the requests of others. There are some ideas about how to strike an appropriate balance later in the chapter.

EMOTIONAL BARRIERS

You know what skills to use, you know what you want, but your emotions get in the way. When emotion mind is in charge, behaviors can be mood-dependent—i.e., we act the way our mood tells us to, not the way our Wise Mind tells us to. Our emotions take over and we do what we feel. It doesn't matter who or what gets in the way, and we can say things that just can't be taken back. It can be super damaging to relationships. To help with this barrier, check your SUDs and look to the crisis survival skills in chapter 5 to lower your SUDs before using interpersonal effectiveness skills. Remember to check in with Wise Mind!

SACRIFICING LONG-TERM GOALS FOR SHORT-TERM GOALS

You may feel strong urges in the short term to avoid or stop an emotion, no matter what the long-term consequences are. Let's say you really hate feeling anxious, and social situations make you anxious, so you avoid them. This type of avoidance is great in the short term because you can avoid your social anxiety. But you also hate feeling lonely, and in the long term, the only thing that will reduce loneliness is making friendships. But how can you work toward creating new friendships? By going into social situations to meet new people who might be potential friends! So, you have to go to the parties, even if they make you anxious in the short term, because it might help fix the long-term problem. Check in with Wise Mind for some help with this barrier.

INTERFERENCE FROM OTHER PEOPLE

You may have the skills to ask for what you want in the most effective way possible, but the problem is the people you are asking are more powerful than you are and maybe they just don't want to say yes. It's disappointing, but it's just the way the world works. The police officer has the power to give you a ticket no matter how compelling your points are about why you don't deserve to get one. Your boss can turn down your request for a raise for all sorts of reasons no matter how great you are at your job. The skills in this chapter make it more likely that folks will say yes to your requests, but they aren't an absolute guarantee. Sometimes it's just out of your control. Look to radical acceptance here (page 77).

BELIEF SYSTEM BARRIERS

All the skills in the world won't help if you have beliefs that get in the way of communicating in the first place. Lots of folks feel like asking for what they want or saying no might result in others being angry or judging them. Others think that people should know what they want without having to be told, and this can certainly get in the way of effective communication. Some think that asking for help indicates they are weak. In any case, beliefs can inhibit being interpersonally effective. Check your facts for some help in overcoming this barrier.

INTERPERSONAL EFFECTIVENESS SKILLS

In this section we'll be looking at the core interpersonal effectiveness skills. It's important to clarify our goals when we're looking at communicating with others. If we're not clear about our goals when communicating with others, things can go off track really fast. One way we can prepare ourselves for meaningful conversations is to ask ourselves three questions:

1. What do I want? What do I want the other person to do, stop doing, take care of, understand, or take seriously as a result of this conversation? Make sure you are as specific as possible. It may be obvious to you, but it's sometimes less obvious to others. The clearer you are, the better. For more on getting what you want, see the DEAR MAN skill (page 105).

2. How do I want the other person to feel about me? This involves how to act in ways that are more likely to result in the other person granting a request, and also balancing immediate goals with the good of the long-term relationship. For example, making threats or demands may get you what you want in the short term, but it usually creates problems in the relationship in the long term. Conversely, always giving in and giving way in relationships usually creates problems over time as well. When

the relationship is important, see Validation (page 108) and GIVE (page 110).

3. How do I want to feel about myself? This involves keeping your self-respect during the interaction. This may include not acting helpless, standing up for yourself, acting with integrity, or maintaining your values. When your self-respect is on the line, see the FAST skill (page 112).

Each of these questions must be considered in interpersonal interactions and may be more or less important in any given conversation. Usually all three are relevant to varying degrees in a particular interaction.

DEAR MAN

When using the DEAR MAN strategy, it's important to know what you want: what your objective is in having the conversation in the first place. Take some time to ask yourself that first question in the list featured on page 117: What do I want? You might even want to talk it over with your therapist or a trusted friend to really get a handle on it. Once you know that answer, then get ready to do some planning. Before you head into a conversation that is important to you, it can be best to write out what you'll say like a script. It helps you really think things through and make plans to cope ahead with emotions that can get in the way of effectively using this conversation strategy.

DESCRIBE

Start by describing the facts of the situation. Keep judgments out of it and stick to the facts. The idea behind this is that stating the facts of the situation gets you and the person you are talking to on the same page with a few specifics that you can both agree on.

Here's an example of a DEAR MAN written by a member of a couple who wants to get the couple's spending on track:

Describe: *"We set up a budget a few months ago and agreed that we would check in with each other on credit card purchases over $75. I went through the credit card bill today and noticed a couple of charges we didn't talk about."*

EXPRESS

Express your feelings about the situation. Don't expect the other person to read your mind or know how you feel just because they know you. This helps the other person understand your point of view. But be brief and don't get lost in your feelings. There's still a long way to go, and this is only the second step.

Express: *"I totally would have agreed with you on buying this stuff. I'm just scared that we are going to get out of the habit of checking in with each other and we could both go back to our old ways of spending without thinking first."*

ASSERT

Here's where you ask for what you want or you say no. Don't beat around the bush or expect others to guess what you want them to do. Be crystal clear.

Assert: *"I would really like to stay firm on our agreement to check in with each other. Can you please continue to check in with me about purchases over $75 even if you are absolutely sure that I will agree that the purchase is necessary?"*

REINFORCE

To reinforce someone means giving them a reward or positive consequence when they do something you want them to do. In this step, you're letting the other person know how they will benefit from granting your request. It's important to really think carefully about what the other person would find reinforcing.

Reinforce: *"I know this is tedious and can feel kind of controlling. But we have talked so much about how we would both* *like to get our spending under control and try to save for a down payment on a house."*

After you complete the DEAR portion, the MAN steps are less about planning what to say in advance, and more about things to keep in mind and ways to respond while delivering your DEAR MAN.

MINDFUL

The important part in staying mindful is not to get distracted by the other person trying to change the subject or making verbal attacks. One technique is "the broken record," which involves simply repeating your request or saying no. The idea is to stay true to your purpose for having the conversation; do not waver and get off track. On your script, you might write some encouraging statements to yourself or some ways you might steer the conversation back to your objective if it goes off track.

(Stay) Mindful: *This is likely to be hard for my partner to hear. They can get super defensive when we talk about money. I will pick my time carefully and not get drawn into an argument. I will keep it easy and breezy. Just a quick reminder of a goal two people who love each other agreed upon for their mutual benefit.*

APPEAR CONFIDENT

Even if you don't feel confident, fake it. Acting more confident can help you feel more confident. Remember, you have a right to ask, even if the other person says no. Check your posture, tone of voice, and eye contact.

Appear confident: *I'm probably going to be a little nervous, so I should probably do some paced breathing and relax my muscles before and during the conversation. I like that little mantra I came up with earlier, as it helps me feel more confident: Just a quick reminder of a goal two people who love each other agreed upon for their mutual benefit.*

Be willing to negotiate and come up with different solutions. Offer to solve the problem in different ways.

Negotiate: *"I'm open to trying different ways to keep our spending under control. It doesn't matter to me how we do it, just that we do it in an effective way."*

Validation

Validation is powerful. It enhances communication, soothes emotions, improves relationships, and builds trust and closeness. It's also a way to regulate emotions. Have you ever been really wound up emotionally and talked to someone who totally understood what you were going thorough? And you found the tension start to flow out of your body and the intensity of your emotion start to reduce? That's the power of validation!

But what is it? Think about it as listening to someone with an accepting and open mind and communicating that open-minded acceptance and understanding of their emotions and experience back to them. Validation is attained not when you *get it*, but when the other person *gets that you get it*. Here's how you do it.

PAY ATTENTION

Pay attention to the person you are attempting to validate. Listen actively, use good eye contact, and reveal with your facial expressions that you are not judging.

REFLECT BACK

Reflect what you heard the other person say to clarify that you understood. You don't have to repeat it exactly, just paraphrase. Let yourself feel some of what the other person is feeling. Let your body posture, voice, and face reflect that. For example: "So you're nervous about the test because you don't think you've studied enough?"

READ MINDS

Read between the lines a bit by paying attention to body language, facial expression, and what you already know about the other person. But don't get too attached to your interpretation; make a gentle guess and ask for confirmation that this assessment is accurate. Let it go if you aren't right. For example: Your partner comes home at the end of a long day and slumps upon entering the kitchen, and you say, "Are you tired? If so, we can order in." Your partner may tell you they are not tired and still want to go out for dinner, or they may confirm your observation and appreciate the opportunity to stay in.

UNDERSTAND

Look for how the other person's feelings, behaviors, or thinking makes sense in light of their life struggles, their recent challenges, or their current state of mind. Strive to get it—even if you don't approve of what they are doing or think their facts aren't right. You do not have to agree with their actions or their facts to empathize with how they feel and understand how they got there. For example: Your friend was recently in a severe car accident. Now she is absolutely terrified when riding as a passenger in the car with you even though you are an excellent driver. Makes sense, considering what she's been through, right? Do you yell at her to chill out? Of course not.

ACKNOWLEDGE THE VALID

If their facts are correct and their behaviors would make sense to anyone, validation gets easier! For example: Your partner is irritated with you because you have forgotten yet again to take out the trash. It is time to validate! "I completely understand why you are annoyed with me. I will take out the trash right now and do my best to take it out in a timelier manner in the future." Now you are a super awesome wonderful partner! Congratulations! (And keep that promise about taking out the trash.)

CONVEY RADICAL EQUALITY/GENUINENESS

Radical genuineness is attempting to understand someone's experience as an equal, not viewing that person as a victim or as different from you. It is respecting and understanding someone's experience on a deeper level. Treat the person as equal in status and respect without being patronizing or condescending. Share the truth of your feelings in a way that shows respect for the other person and yourself.

GIVE

The GIVE skill is all about keeping and maintaining relationships. You will want to ask yourself the second question from the list on page 117: How do I want the other person to feel about me? This skill is about how you treat the other person while you deliver your DEAR MAN or just while you interact with other folks in general. One benefit is that people are often more likely to give us what we want when we are nice to them. Another is that we generally feel better about ourselves when we treat others in a kinder, more compassionate way.

(BE) GENTLE

Remember that you might actually care about this relationship, this person, this human. Be nice. No attacks or threats. Steer clear of judgments. If you are telling someone that you must make changes in the relationship if they don't do something differently, stick to the facts and stay gentle in your approach. For example: "I would like you not to visit me at work anymore. In fact, I would like you to not visit me at all wearing a bear costume. It scares people, and I find it embarrassing." This sends a firm message in a gentler tone than, "Hey, freak, cut it out with the bear thing. You look like a lunatic. If you ever so much as think of wearing a bear costume again, I will kick your butt from here to New Jersey. What the heck is wrong with you?"

(ACT) INTERESTED

Listen to the other person. Don't assume you know what their responses will be or that you already know what they will say. Occasionally, you will need to listen to someone far longer or after they have gotten the message across, or you will need to listen to them talk about something that is not important to you. That's why the skill is (act) interested, not (be) interested. In any relationship, you just sometimes have to listen to someone talk about something you find boring and tedious.

VALIDATE

Keep in mind the validation skills you learned earlier in this chapter (page 108). Here's one more idea about validation. Functional validation is showing someone that you take them seriously with your actions. If someone is crying, hand them a tissue. If someone says they are hungry, get them some food. If someone says they need space, give them some time alone. We can all talk the talk. Functional validation is about walking the walk.

EASY MANNER

Have an easy manner. Try to be lighthearted and maybe even be a little humorous if it is appropriate. Try to make the situation more comfortable, not so serious and intense. I often find that when people are having difficult conversations, they speak as if the entire world was about to end, when in reality, we are all ultimately going to be okay after even the most difficult interactions. Even the smallest acknowledgment of that—maybe using a pet name with a loved one, or avoiding the "we need to talk" tone of voice—can help.

FAST

The FAST skill is intended to be used when you need to make sure you walk away from an interaction feeling like you behaved with integrity, that you maintained your self-respect. The question you are answering here is: How do I want to feel about myself? Did I get what I wanted by lying or making threats, or did I get what I wanted by being fair and sticking to my values?

FAIR

The important thing here is to not only be fair to yourself but also to the other person. It is hard to respect yourself if you take advantage of other people. On the other hand, always giving in to others and never standing up for yourself can make it hard to respect yourself, too. Trying to be fair helps you maintain your self-respect.

(NO) APOLOGIES

This doesn't mean never apologize. If you've done something wrong, of course you should apologize. This skill is about over-apologizing—for living, for breathing, for having needs, for taking up space, for asking for anything, or for saying no. You have a right to ask for things and to say no. Also, constantly apologizing can be pretty annoying to others and can negatively impact relationships. So can constantly asking others if they are mad at you, so avoid that, too.

STICK TO YOUR VALUES

Avoid selling out or changing your values or opinions in order to keep another person liking you. It's difficult to hold your own values when you struggle with feeling horrible, when you think others are judging you for your beliefs, or you feel you don't necessarily have a right to your own beliefs.

TRUTHFUL

Try to develop a pattern of honesty in your relationships. Don't act helpless when you are not, and work toward mastery rather than trying to get others to take care of things for you. Try not to exaggerate or make up excuses.

DBT IN ACTION: DEAR MAN

Danielle was struggling at work even though she was quite good at her job. Whenever an assignment was difficult or required extra work, it was automatically assigned to her because the bosses knew she could handle it. The easier stuff went to her coworkers, because they just weren't as skilled. Danielle was flattered. She knew she would get a promotion eventually, but in the meantime, she was feeling pretty burned out and needed her bosses to hear her ideas about how the work could be more evenly distributed.

Danielle crafted her DEAR MAN to focus on asking her bosses to consider allowing her to train her peers to take on some of the harder tasks. She did her homework and created a time-limited training schedule that would bring her peers up to speed relatively quickly on several key tasks. She wanted to clearly express a few things: although she had accepted the work up until this point without complaint, the job in the way it was currently structured was not sustainable; she would need to look for other work unless changes were made; and she really wanted to stay, as she saw her future with this organization.

She wrote up her DEAR MAN. She knew that GIVE was going to be important. She had developed a close relationship with her bosses and knew the pressure they were under. She could easily validate that the change she was suggesting was going to take effort, flexibility, and creativity to accomplish. She also knew FAST was vital. Her self-respect was at stake. It was in her nature to suck it up and get the work done. She knew herself well enough that this would lead her to feeling resentful, and she didn't want that.

HOW INTERPERSONAL EFFECTIVENESS SKILLS WORK TOGETHER

So you see, there's a pretty delicate balance going on here. To get what you want, you prepare a DEAR MAN. While you are delivering the DEAR MAN, you balance GIVE skills to maintain the relationship and FAST skills to maintain your self-respect. Every interaction is different, and every time there's a different balance necessary.

Sometimes getting what you want is the most important thing. So you might think, "Hey, I just do a DEAR MAN, right? Don't worry about GIVE or FAST." But you'll find, depending on each interaction, it can be most effective to draw from all of the interpersonal effectiveness skills. And no matter what, validation, the V in GIVE, is always the sugar that helps the medicine go down. When done well, it will enhance any interaction. You might think that talking to the airport staff about your messed-up plane reservation might not require GIVE, but if they had been screamed at all day, your GIVE to that staff member might get you on a plane that day.

Using GIVE and FAST Together

Often when folks are trying to stand up for themselves and trying to maintain their self-respect, they think they can't blend the FAST and GIVE skills. They think they can't be gentle or have an easy manner while still holding firm on setting a limit with someone else. But it is possible. In fact, it can often be the most effective way to do so. Validating the other person's emotions, desires, or point of view while still maintaining your own limits is a way to help the other person see that you are taking their point of view seriously, which may help them take yours more seriously as well.

Using Other Skills Along with Interpersonal Effectiveness Skills

Being emotionally regulated prior to using interpersonal effectiveness skills is important. Check your SUDs and use mindfulness and distress tolerance skills to get your SUDs down before you try to deliver a DEAR MAN. Cope ahead—the C from ABC PLEASE—is a perfect skill for using with DEAR MAN, GIVE, and FAST. Vividly imagine yourself managing well in a difficult interpersonal situation. Using all the skills and dealing effectively is a great way to practice before you go into an important conversation.

And finally, you can always DEAR the DEAR MAN. What on earth does this mean? If the whole conversation is just falling apart and going wrong and everything is blowing up, you can use DEAR to either turn the conversation around or end the conversation in order to try again later. It can go something like this:

Describe. *It's hard for me to stay in this conversation when things are getting so heated.*

Express. *I feel overwhelmed and anxious.*

Assert. *Let's take some time to cool down.*

Reinforce. *I think if we keep going, this is going to turn into an argument, and neither of us wants that. If we come back to this later, we will have had some time to come up with other ideas that may solve the problem.*

KEY TAKEAWAYS

We've covered a lot of ways to communicate in this chapter. You've learned how to make it more likely to get what you want, and how to communicate in ways that can keep your relationships stronger and maintain your self-respect. As we move forward, it will be helpful to keep in mind:

→ Remember to be clear about your goal(s) before you attempt to enter into a significant communication. To do so, ask yourself these questions:

  → What do I want?

  → How do I want the other person to feel about me?

  → How do I want to feel about myself?

→ When planning a DEAR MAN, write it out in script form so that you can think carefully about what you would like to say and how you would like to say it.

→ Validation is communication magic. When someone understands that you understand and accept their experience, it enhances relationships and builds trust. You can even validate yourself!

CHAPTER 8

Putting DBT into Practice

We've spent the last four chapters learning the basic DBT skills. In this, our final chapter, we'll look at the tools that therapists and clients can use to measure, track, analyze, and create new solutions for emotions, behaviors, and skills use. You'll also learn how to increase and maintain your motivation and commitment to treatment and ongoing skills use.

DBT FAST FACTS:
LET'S MAKE SOME CHEAT SHEETS

You may have started wondering, "How on earth am I supposed to remember all of these skills?" That's a really good point. There are a lot of skills, and it can be hard to remember skills when your SUDs are high. That's part of why DBT depends so much on acronyms: to help jog memory.

Think about what works best for you when you need to recall information in a high-pressure situation, like an exam. For me, it's cheat sheets: letter-size sheets of paper with important information written in different colors on different parts of the page. Somehow, my recall is better because I can see the color and where the info is on the page in my mind's eye.

For others it's 3x5 flash cards, either paper or digital. Others talk out the skills into the voice recorder on their phone and listen to the playback. Others label skillful behavior as they see it in real life or on television. Some put the skills on sticky notes on their bathroom mirror and read them while they brush their teeth. Some teach the skills to loved ones to further embed them in their minds. What works for you?

TRACKING EMOTIONS AND URGES

For folks with big emotional responses, traditional weekly talk therapy can easily be derailed, with no ill intent on the part of anyone involved. Because things often feel like crises, longer-term goals can fall by the wayside, important items to be addressed can be missed, and there is little to no time to learn skills or make strides that lead to a life worth living because there is a problem that *feels* like it must be solved right now.

Memory gets in the way here, too. Let's say you had strong urges to engage in self-destructive behavior earlier in the week. But, the morning of your therapy session, you have a rip-roaring argument with your sister. What's going to be freshest in your mind? That fight with your sister, for sure. So that's what you talk about in your session. But which topic really needs to be addressed first? The self-destructive behavior, of course! But that's not what *feels* most pressing right now, it is only a faded memory.

And let's say the self-destructive urges keep occurring, but you don't bring them up for a few weeks because some other difficult event keeps cropping up nearer to the time of each session. Those self-destructive urges just aren't at the forefront of your mind when you sit down across from your therapist. But they sure hit hard at 2:00 a.m. when you're all alone, feeling miserable and hopeless. Finally, one night you get super scared, and you call your therapist asking for help. She gets upset when she finds these urges have been quite overwhelming for some time. Just not at therapy time.

The desire to make sure that therapy stays on track and addresses the most urgent behaviors in real time leads us to another flash of brilliance from our beloved Dr. Marsha Linehan. Behold, the diary card.

Keeping a Diary Card

The diary card is a behavior-tracking tool used by most DBT therapists and their clients. The diary card is intended to make sure that that 2:00 a.m. behavior that gets in the way of your life being worth living is attended to during each session as needed. Most diary cards already have sections prefilled out for suicidal ideation and self-harm urges and actions, along with several spaces for other behaviors that folks are working on decreasing (or in some cases increasing).

There are also spaces for you to note items you would like to add to the therapy agenda for that week. The idea is that you mindfully fill out your diary card daily and present it to your therapist during your weekly session. Then, you and your therapist can determine the behaviors that need the most attention, typically according to the DBT hierarchy of treatment: life-threatening behaviors (suicidal ideation and attempts and self-harm), then therapy-interfering behaviors, then behaviors that interfere with quality of life, then skill building. Generally, you and your therapist will do behavior chain analysis and solution analysis (not just crisis management) around behaviors that get in the way of your life worth living (more about this in just a few sections!).

Tracking Emotions and Skills Use

Also on the diary card, there will be areas for tracking your emotions. Tracking emotions will help you become better at accurately identifying your emotions and tying them to events throughout your week. You won't only be tracking negative emotions though; you will also be tracking positive emotions. So, the diary card can also help you identify activities and situations that bring you joy and happiness as well as remind you that when things are not so great you actually do have fun sometimes. Daily, mindfully, reflecting and recording your range of emotions allows you to get a much better sense of how, why, and when emotions fire for you, which is a big part of learning how to regulate them.

Also on a typical diary card, there is a list of the DBT skills. The idea here is to track your skills use: When you are using skills, which ones, how often, and how effective each skill is in the situations you are using them for. This helps you identify your go-to skills—the ones that are most effective for you and the ones that you can depend on when things hit the fan. This tracking also helps you identify the skills you need to improve upon—i.e., the ones that maybe you need to clarify a bit more about how to use or when not to use to get more mileage out of them. Tracking even helps you understand why you may be thinking about but not using skills when you need to.

You may be wondering, "Where can I get one of these diary cards you speak of"? A Google search for DBT Diary Card will pull up a bunch. I have a link to one I use with instructions for filling it out in the Resources section of this book. You can also find helpful diary card apps in the app store on your smartphone by searching DBT Diary Card.

ANALYZING BEHAVIOR

While Nancy Reagan was First Lady, she launched a program intended to stop kids from using drugs. It was called "Just Say No." The idea was that if you were a child of the 1980s and someone offered you drugs or alcohol, you would be taught to avoid drug misuse and potential addiction by simply saying no. Problem solved.

Turns out, for a lot of people, resisting the lure of substances (just like many other behaviors that can make us feel good in the short term but can create major problems in the long run) is a whole lot more complicated than just saying no. There are all kinds of reasons why people engage in behaviors that aren't good for them in the long term. And my reasons for engaging in these behaviors, the situations that I find emotionally dysregulating, and the consequences of my behaviors are likely to be different from your reasons, behaviors, situations, and consequences. That's why being able to understand our own behavior in varying situations is so vitally important. How we do that is by looking at a specific series of events like detectives, searching for clues as to how the series of events will play out.

Behavior Chain Analysis

Behavior chain analysis is most often done in individual DBT therapy but can be a valuable tool to learn to do for yourself.

As you and your therapist do the detective work, each clue in the series of events is a link in the chain of events that brings you closer to understanding what leads to a specific behavior. You look at each of these links in the chain to figure out what the problem behavior is, what prompts the problem behavior, the function of the problem behavior, and what consequences keep the problem behavior in place. You'll do a solution analysis to figure out where to insert DBT skills in the chain to know what to do next time to avoid the problem behavior.

You know when you watch a detective show and you see the evidence wall with all of the information about the unsolved case pinned up so that the detective can solve the crime? Chain analysis is kind of like that. It's often done visually; you'll usually see a preponderance of whiteboards in offices devoted to DBT treatment, and getting a chain analysis up on the board is the reason why. Getting a chain down on paper is helpful, too; I've included links to DBT sites that offer chain analysis and solution analysis in the Resources section of this book.

Some clients can feel like they are being punished by having to do a chain analysis, by having to go over a problem behavior with their therapist that they may already be ashamed of having done in the first place. Please remember that the spirit of a chain analysis is intended to be that of discovery and problem solving, not shaming and pointing out where you went wrong. Remember: if these problem behaviors were easy to solve, you would have figured them out long ago. That's why they require such an in-depth analysis. Here are the elements of a chain analysis:

IDENTIFY THE PROBLEM BEHAVIOR

Describe the behavior in a specific, detailed way. Pretend you are a screenwriter and you are giving directions to the actor who will play the part.

Problem Behavior: I drunk texted my ex-boyfriend asking to get back together.

VULNERABILITY FACTORS

These are things in your life that make you more vulnerable to reacting in more problematic ways, usually stuff within the last 24 to 48 hours, but they can also be ongoing stressors. Things that can make you vulnerable include illness, poor eating or sleeping, substance use, intense emotions, or stressful events.

Vulnerability Factors: I got yelled at while I was at work. I skipped lunch and had two drinks at happy hour on an empty stomach.

PROMPTING EVENT

This is the event that set off the chain of events leading to the problem behavior. Think of it as the last straw on the camel's back—that if that specific event had not occurred, the problem behavior probably would not have occurred. The prompting event can be either internal (thoughts, memories, flashbacks, feelings) or external (something in your environment, someone saying or doing something).

Prompting Event: I met my friend for happy hour and was having a really good time. A guy came up and hit on her and she asked me if it was okay if she left with him.

LINKS IN THE CHAIN

Here's where you describe the events between the prompting event and the problem behavior. Each of these links in the chain are important. Links are generally comprised of the following categories: actions (things you do); body sensations (things you feel in your body); thoughts (including expectations, judgments, etc.); events in the environment (including things others do); and emotions (yours, not others).

Links: My heart started racing, and I felt tears in my eyes (body sensations). I pretended I was okay and told my friend to go and have fun (actions). On my drive home, I felt angry (emotion) because I thought my friend wanted to spend time with me, and it turned out she was more interested in some random guy (thoughts). Then, I felt ashamed (emotion) because I felt bad about being angry at my friend. My SUDs were very high, and I wanted to do anything not to feel that way. I had a bottle of wine in the refrigerator and ended up drinking the whole thing (action). While I drank that, I started feeling lonely (emotion) and thinking about how I will always be alone, especially because guys never come up to me in bars (thoughts). My phone went off with a text from my friend saying how much she liked the guy from the bar (environment). I started crying (action) and felt like there was a giant burning hole in my chest (body sensation). It occurred to me that a crappy boyfriend was better than none at all (thought) and looked up my ex's number in my phone (action).

CONSEQUENCES

Consequences are what happens because of the problem behavior. These consequences can be either positive or negative. Often, the immediate consequences are positive in some way; that's what helps keep problematic behaviors in place.

Consequences: My ex seemed happy to hear from me, and we made plans to get together the next day. This made me feel less lonely and scared for my future, so it was positive, at least in the moment. The next morning, I woke up really hungover, which was negative. When I remembered that I had a lunch date with my ex, I totally panicked. It had taken a lot of time and effort to break off the relationship, as my ex can be invalidating, and it can be tough to get him to see my point of view. I felt really guilty, because giving my ex hope that we would get back together was against my values.

Solution Analysis

In the chain analysis we found out what happened and gained a lot of information about the factors contributing to the problem behavior. So now what do we do? It's time for a solution analysis! This is when we apply DBT skills to the behavioral chain so that in future similar situations we know how we can manage in more effective ways. We can apply skills to most elements of a chain; let's see how we can apply skills to our previous example. The idea here is that at any point in the chain, a skills application can break the chain and stop the problem behavior from happening. As you are looking at this solution analysis, you can see there are skills to do to make sure the problem doesn't happen again, and there are skills to repair damage done.

In the previous example, let's look at how to address the vulnerability factors:

→ *Yelled at while at work: may need to do a chain to get more info*

→ *Skipped lunch: PLEASE skill—balanced eating. What snacks can I keep in my desk if I can't manage my time to get out for lunch?*

→ *Two drinks at happy hour on an empty stomach: PLEASE skill—avoid mood-altering substances, or balance eating (bar snacks!)*

Let's look at how to address the prompting event:

→ *My friend met a guy at happy hour and left with him instead of staying with me: DEAR MAN with GIVE and FAST to ask my friend to keep girls' night out just to us girls before we go out again*

Let's look at how to address the links in the chain:

→ *Racing heart, tears in eyes (paced breathing)*

→ *"My friend is more interested in some random guy than spending time with me." (access Wise Mind, check the facts)*

→ *Angry, ashamed, very high SUDs, wine will lower my SUDs (crisis survival skills—especially the TIPP skills)*

→ *Lonely, "I will always be alone, especially because guys never come up to me in bars." (crisis survival skills—let's do ACCEPTS this time to distract from the emotion and the thought, as both are just unhelpful right now. I could check the facts, but I might be too much in emotion mind to do this right now.)*

→ *Text from my friend about guy from bar, crying, felt like there was a giant burning hole in my chest (body sensation) (How about some more crisis survival skills? Let's do self-soothing this time—might help with that burning pain in the chest.)*

→ *It occurred to me that a crappy boyfriend was better than none at all (thought) and looked up my ex's number in my phone (action). (Let's get mindful here—and bring Wise Mind on board. A pros and cons list could be pretty helpful here!)*

Finally, let's apply skills to the consequences:

→ *Made plans to get together the next day with my ex. (Make a pros and cons list to remind my future self why contact with my ex is a bad idea.)*

→ *Giving my ex hope that we would get back together was against my values. (Draft a DEAR MAN to apologize, as well as to set limits about future contact and cope ahead to be able to deliver it effectively.)*

Missing Links Analysis

When effective behavior was needed or expected and didn't occur, a "missing links analysis" is called for. It's a series of four questions that can help you understand how and why behaviors aren't happening.

So, when an effective behavior did not occur, you can ask:

1. Did you know what effective behavior was needed? If not, figure out what gets in the way. How can you find out this information?

2. Were you willing to do the effective behavior? If not, consider building your skills in the areas of radical acceptance, turning the mind, and opposite action.

3. Did the thought of doing the effective behavior ever enter your mind? If not, how can you make this front of mind when you need it? Can you set an alarm, put it on a calendar, or practice coping ahead?

4. What got in the way of doing the effective behavior? Was it procrastination due to mood-dependent behavior? Thinking no one would find out? Consider pros and cons lists, practicing opposite action, setting up a reward system for yourself, or having an accountability partner.

DBT IN ACTION: SKILLS PLAN

It was Dave's final night in DBT skills group. He would have his last session with his DBT therapist tomorrow. Dave had all of his life-threatening and therapy-interfering behaviors under control. He and his DBT therapist had made a list of behaviors that interfere with quality of life that Dave would continue to focus on through weekly sessions with a DBT-informed therapist and skills plans Dave had created with his DBT therapist. He had a good plan. He was nervous but ready.

Dave asked the group leaders for permission to lead the mindfulness activity. He asked the participants to take a moment and make a list of everything they were grateful for in the group room. He then asked the participants to share their lists if they felt comfortable doing so. Dave then thanked the other participants and the group leaders for their role in his DBT journey. He told them about the times he had been disheartened and someone in group had a success that had helped him recommit. He mentioned when the group leaders helped him understand skills in ways that hadn't made sense to him before.

The next day he had his final meeting with his DBT therapist. They talked about how far he had come. They reviewed those skills plans one last time. They agreed that Dave had a good plan. He was ready.

MAINTAINING MOTIVATION

Staying the course in DBT treatment requires the motivation to do the treatment, to use skills, and to make big changes in how you think about and do all kinds of things. It's a big commitment of time and energy, and, often money. You bet finding and maintaining motivation is important!

Identifying your reasons for doing DBT is vital to finding, keeping, and maintaining your motivation. As you have read, DBT was originally created for chronically suicidal and self-harming patients. Dr. Marsha Linehan knew that keeping these folks alive just wasn't enough; she would have to help them build lives that they experienced as worth living. In DBT world, everyone, suicidal or not, is working on the goal of building a life worth living. The question is: What are the components of a life that is meaningful and important to you, that you experience as worth living?

When thinking about your life worth living, think of friendships, romantic relationships, family, education, work, meaningful pastimes, and how or where you want to live. If you struggle with believing it's possible for you to achieve your goals, hopes, or aspirations, or you struggle with whether you deserve a life worth living, it's okay to keep the goal on the more modest side, but I hope you'll adjust as you build mastery. We might each have our personal limitations, but we can all build a life we experience as worth living.

How to Stay Focused on Your Goals

You may have noticed that we have lots of goals going on in DBT, and truthfully, it can get pretty confusing. Looking at goals this way can help:

All goals in DBT are in service of building the goal of a life worth living.

INDIVIDUAL THERAPY	SKILLS TRAINING GROUP	BETWEEN SESSION COACHING
Life-threatening and self-harming behaviors are always the goals attended to first in individual therapy, because you can't have a life worth living if you are in danger of dying.	DBT skills are taught and practiced in a group setting throughout treatment. Skills are meant to stop and reduce life-threatening, therapy-interfering behavior and behavior that interferes with quality of life. As well as support behaviors that help build a life worth living.	When assistance is needed in using skills out in the real world, between-sessions phone coaching fits the bill. Being able to be skillful in real time helps you meet your therapeutic goals and build a life worth living.
Reducing therapy-interfering behaviors is the next goal attended to in individual therapy, because if you aren't getting the treatment you need, you are unlikely to build your life worth living.		
Reducing behaviors that interfere with quality of life (mental health symptoms, substance abuse, eating disorders, relationship difficulties, etc.) is the set of goals that are addressed next, as they interfere with building a life worth living.		

Reminding yourself of your goal to have a life worth living is a way to stay focused and maintain motivation in DBT.

CHOOSE YOUR GOALS USING WISE MIND

As you are determining goals for yourself, you might find emotion mind showing up. Sometimes, you might think that you don't have to focus on a certain behavior because you did that for the last time a few days ago and you feel sure you will never do it again. Check in with Wise Mind. Wise Mind is likely to tell you that behavior still needs to be focused on.

After doing DBT for a while, you may feel like DBT isn't working for you. That may be true. Or it may not be. Make sure to talk to your therapist, review the progress on your diary cards, make pros and cons lists, and have a check-in with Wise Mind.

SET INTERMEDIATE GOALS

Remember, small steps. Give yourself the satisfaction of reaching smaller goals along the way to larger goals. You know how good it feels to cross something off your to-do list? Ever been tempted to put extra items on your list just to have the satisfaction of crossing them off? Smaller goals are kind of like that; they give us a little buzz of accomplishment while letting us know we are on the right path.

REMIND YOURSELF OF YOUR SUCCESSES

I know someone who loves her to-do lists. But she loves her completed to-do lists even more. She calls them ta-done lists (kind of like a mix of "ta-da" and "to-do") and puts them up to remind herself how productive and accomplished she has been. How can you remind yourself of your small successes along the way toward your larger goals?

SURROUND YOURSELF WITH SUPPORTIVE PEOPLE (AND DISTANCE YOURSELF FROM THOSE WHO AREN'T)

Sometimes folks are going to be all about the new, more skillful you. They are going to be your biggest cheerleaders and supporters. If you are in a DBT skills group, you already have a group of people who are pulling for you to succeed. Other times, there may be folks who have a hard time knowing how to support you. If using your interpersonal effectiveness skills to educate those folks doesn't make a difference, distancing yourself so that you can continue on your path toward your life worth living may be your only choice.

Tips for Staying Motivated

Changing behavior is hard, and staying motivated can be difficult. Sometimes you don't feel like using skills. Sometimes you start to doubt if working so hard is worth it. You may even, in emotion mind, start to doubt that DBT can help you, even though you have lots of evidence to the contrary. Here are some more ways to keep going when motivation is flagging.

KEEP LONG-TERM GOALS IN MIND

Keep going back to that goal to have a life worth living. Check in regularly with Wise Mind and make sure you are on track. Make visual or physical reminders of your larger goals to remind you. Check in with people you respect and review your goals. Refine them from time to time. Recognize the small bit of progress toward your larger goals to make them more real in the day-to-day.

USE YOUR EXPERIENCES AS LEARNING OPPORTUNITIES

When times get tough, it can be hard to see the upside. One way to look at setbacks and challenges is to see them as an opportunity to build mastery by using skills. Another way is proving to yourself that you can do hard things and still manage. These experiences will still be difficult, but viewing them as also being learning opportunities can make them at least have some meaning.

PRACTICE PATIENCE

A big part of regulating emotions is slowing down and getting better at feeling the emotions we don't want to feel in the service of finding out that they actually aren't so horrifically intolerable after all. Not that they aren't sucky and unpleasant, as they certainly are. But difficult emotions can be survived. Any practice we can get in building patience can only help with that. The point is that achieving your goals takes time. Quitting is fast, but then you don't achieve your goals. So, practice patience. Progress may be slower than you like. But at least you are on your way.

KEY TAKEAWAYS

This, our final chapter together, has been all about how to stay focused and motivated in achieving goals in DBT. We've explored the motivation of building toward a life worth living. You've learned about the diary card and how it helps us stay focused on those important-to-address behaviors that might slip through the cracks. You've seen the power of behavior chain and solution analysis in learning to manage problematic behaviors. As you move forward, it will be helpful to keep in mind:

→ Chain analysis and solution analysis are powerful tools that some folks avoid because they feel shame at having engaged in a problematic behavior. Do them anyway. They are incredibly helpful in understanding and solving the factors that lead to behaviors that get in the way of your life worth living.

→ Doing a diary card daily gives you time to reflect on your day and take stock. It is very helpful in keeping your progress in DBT on track. It takes very little time to fill out and has a big payoff.

→ The ultimate aim of DBT is to build a life worth living. Consider the factors that make up your life worth living.

Looking Forward

We've talked about dialectics and how DBT treats emotion dysregulation. We've looked at how DBT is structured so that you can make the best choices in identifying appropriate treatment providers. We've covered the four modules of DBT—Mindfulness, Distress Tolerance, Emotion Regulation, and Interpersonal Effectiveness. Finally, we've looked at the importance of tracking and analyzing behavior and maintaining motivation.

Along the way, I hope you've sampled what I've presented of DBT. Whether you are someone who struggles with managing your emotions, love someone who does, or are a therapist, the best way to learn DBT is by doing it. So, put those skills to work, over and over again.

And yes, if you struggle with emotion dysregulation, getting professional, qualified DBT therapy is the best option; do so if you possibly can. If you want to be a DBT therapist, excellent training is available. If you are a loved one, there are exceptional resources available for you.

I want to remind you that this book has only covered a very brief review of the major components of DBT. There is still so much left to learn, so check out the Resources section for suggestions on additional information.

Glossary

behavior chain analysis: This is a method by which a therapist and client analyze and seek to understand all of the variables that contribute to a problem behavior occurring and staying in place.

biosocial theory: This is a transactional theory that attempts to explain why some people have such a hard time managing their emotions and behaviors.

dialectics: This is the idea that two opposing viewpoints can both hold truth at the same time.

diary card: This is a tracking device that allows clients to monitor their emotions, skills use, and target behaviors between sessions to provide important information to address during each individual therapy session.

emotional avoidance: This refers to intentional and unintentional behaviors engaged in to avoid feeling difficult emotions (for example, avoiding a friend you have wronged in order to avoid feeling guilty).

emotion dysregulation: This refers to the difficulty of managing emotions when they occur. Sometimes this involves being unable to identify your emotions, respond effectively to them, and deal with the aftermath of an emotion.

justified emotion: This is an emotion that fits the facts of a situation (for example, feeling scared when there is a threat to your well-being).

mood-dependent behavior: This refers to engaging in a behavior because you feel like it, even if that behavior does not fit in with your short-term and long-term goals (for example, staying in bed rather than going to class even though getting a degree is important to you).

reality acceptance: This refers to choosing to accept what is happening in this moment rather than thinking about what "should" be happening. For example, accepting that traffic is heavier in the morning and allowing for it rather than saying it "should" only take twenty minutes to get to work and often feeling rushed and late.

self-dysregulation: This is a sense of emptiness, a lack of a sense of self, or feeling alone and misunderstood despite attempts to fit in.

solution analysis: This is an analysis of a chain of events leading to a problem behavior, with DBT skills attached to each link in the chain in order to have a plan for the next time a similar chain of events occurs.

subjective units of distress scale (SUDs): This is a rating scale (usually from 0 to 10 or 0 to 100—with 0 being no distress) that allows a person to rate their own subjective level of distress in a particular situation.

unjustified emotion: This is when an emotion does not fit the facts of a given situation, either because of the situation itself, the time the emotion lasts, or its intensity. For example, if I am still feeling a high level of fear following my child sneaking up and saying "BOO" to me twenty minutes after the event, that would not be a justified emotion.

Resources

Finding Certified DBT Providers

Behavioral Tech

BehavioralTech.org/resources/find-a-therapist

Here you will find a listing of clinicians who are certified in DBT by the DBT-Linehan Board of Certification (DBT-LBC).

Apps

Calm

Calm.com

Calm is an award-winning mindfulness app featuring hundreds of calming exercises, helpful breathing techniques, and sleep stories.

DBT Coach

Resiliens.com

This is an app that allows you to learn, practice, and track your DBT skills use.

DBT Diary Card and Skills App

DiaryCard.net

This is an app designed by a licensed psychologist. It has a DBT reference section as well as a fillable diary card you can send to your therapist.

Headspace

Headspace.com

Headspace has meditation and mindfulness practices for all kinds of moods and situations.

Insight Timer
InsightTimer.com
This is another mindfulness and meditation app. There are many teachers, and you may choose one that resonates with you.

Books

The Borderline Personality Disorder Survival Guide: Everything You Need to Know About Living with BPD by Alexander L. Chapman and Kim L. Gratz

Building a Life Worth Living by Marsha M. Linehan

The High-Conflict Couple: A Dialectical Behavior Therapy Guide to Finding Peace, Intimacy and Validation by Alan E. Fruzzetti

Loving Someone with Borderline Personality Disorder by Shari Manning

The Mindfulness Solution for Intense Emotions: Take Control of Borderline Personality Disorder with DBT by Cedar Koons

The Miracle of Mindfulness by Thich Nhất Hanh

Mindfulness for Borderline Personality Disorder: Relieve Your Suffering Using the Core Skill of Dialectical Behavior Therapy by Blaise Aguirre and Gillian Galen

Websites

BorderlinePersonalityDisorder.org/family-connections
This is the website for the National Education Alliance for Borderline Personality Disorder's Family Connections program, a twelve-week evidence-based program for loved ones of folks

who struggle with emotion dysregulation. The website in general is a treasure trove of information about BPD.

DBTselfhelp.com
A website created and maintained by DBT users, not professionals.

HopeForBPD.com/my-dialectical-life-dbt-selfhelp
A subscription service for an emailed DBT skill of the day.

Training for Therapists

Behavioral Tech

BehavioralTech.org/training/training-catalog

Mammalian Dive Reflex

YouTube.com/watch?v=tVqw5HnJg-g

Psychwire

Psychwire.com/linehan/courses

Treatment Implementation Collaborative

TICllc.org

References

Bailey, Alyssa. "Selena Gomez on Her Mental Health Journey, DBT Changing Her Life, and Turning 29." *ELLE*. November 29, 2021. Elle.com/culture/celebrities/a36799996/selena -gomez-mental-health-dbt-29th-birthday-interview.

"Core Evidence and Research." Behavioral Tech. BehavioralTech .org/research/evidence.

"For What Conditions Is DBT Effective?" Behavioral Tech. BehavioralTech.org/research/evidence.

Frazier, Savannah N., and Jamie Vela. "Dialectical Behavior Therapy for the Treatment of Anger and Aggressive Behavior: A Review." *Aggression and Violent Behavior* 19, no. 2 (March/ April 2014): 156–63. doi:10.1016/j.avb.2014.02.001.

Fruzzetti, Alan E. *The High-Conflict Couple: A Dialectical Behavior Therapy Guide to Finding Peace, Intimacy, and Validation*. Oakland, CA: New Harbinger Publications, Inc., 2006.

Harned, Melanie S., Safia C. Jackson, Katherine A. Comtois, and Marsha M. Linehan. "Dialectical Behavior Therapy as a Precursor to PTSD Treatment for Suicidal and/or Self-Injuring Women with Borderline Personality Disorder." *Journal of Traumatic Stress* 23, no. 4 (2010): 421–29. doi:10.1002/jts.20553.

Linehan, Marsha M. *DBT Skills Training Manual, 2nd edition.* New York: Guilford Press, 2015.

—— *DBT Skills Training Handouts and Worksheets, 2nd edition.* New York: Guilford Press, 2015.

—— *Building a Life Worth Living: A Memoir.* New York: Random House, 2020.

Mazza, James J., Elizabeth T. Dexter-Mazza, Alec L. Miller, Jill H. Rathus, and Heather E. Murphy. *DBT Skills in Schools: Skills Training for Emotional Problem Solving for Adolescents (DBT STEPS-A)* New York: Guilford Press, 2016.

Neacsiu, Andrada D., Jeremy W. Eberle, Rachel Kramer, Taylor Wiesmann, and Marsha M. Linehan. "Dialectical Behavior Therapy Skills for Transdiagnostic Emotion Dysregulation: A Pilot Randomized Controlled Trial." *Behaviour Research and Therapy* 59 (2014): 40–51. doi:10.1016/j.brat.2014.05.005.

Sauter, Disa A., Frank Eisner, Andrew J. Calder, and Sophie K. Scott. "Perceptual Cues in Nonverbal Vocal Expressions of Emotion." *Quarterly Journal of Experimental Psychology* 63, no. 11 (November 2010): 2251–72. doi:10.1080/17470211003721642.

Stiglmayr, Christian, Julia Stecher-Mohr, Till Wagner, Jeannette Meißner, Doreen Spretz, Christiane Steffens, Stefan Roepke, et al. "Effectiveness of Dialectic Behavioral Therapy in Routine Outpatient Care: The Berlin Borderline Study." *Borderline Personality Disorder and Emotion Dysregulation* 1, no. 1 (September 2015): 20. doi:10.1186/2051-6673-1-20.

Stuntz, Elizabeth C., and Marsha M. Linehan. *Coping with Cancer: DBT Skills to Manage Your Emotions—and Balance Uncertainty with Hope*. New York: Guilford Press, 2021.

Winfrey, Oprah. "Lady Gaga Opens up to Oprah about Trauma, Self-Harm, and Choosing Kindness." *ELLE*. February 17, 2021. Elle.com/culture/music/a29683686/lady-gaga -haus-laboratories-elle-interview/.

Index

Crisis Survival skills
  crisis survival kits, 76, 80
  describing and defining, 8, 64–65
  IMPROVE-ing the
    moment, 69, 73–75
  impulsive behaviors,
    curbing with, 67–68
  pros and cons, use of, 68,
    69–71, 76, 128, 133
  SUDs, using with high
    levels of, 80, 102
  TIPP your body chemistry,
    68, 71–73, 76, 128

D
DEAR MAN skill
  DEAR the DEAR MAN
    technique, 116
  drafting of letter, 114, 115, 117, 128
  getting what you want with, 104
  skill in delivering, 110
  in solution analysis, 127
  strategy, describing and
    defining, 105–108
Depression, 2, 12, 39, 57
Describing skill, 53
*Diagnostic and Statistical
  Manual of Mental Disorders
  (DSM)*, 36, 38, 48
Dialectical Abstinence, 13
Dialectical Behavior Therapy (DBT)
  all sides, practice in looking at, 6
  behavioral health concerns,
    supporting, 2, 14
  biosocial theory, 33–36, 41, 44, 140
  BPD, success in treating
    with, 12–13
  cheat sheet for DBT
    acronyms, 120
  DBT notebook, creating, 26–27
  describing and defining, 3–4, 15
  emotional dysregulation,
    helping with, 10, 11

five functions of DBT
  treatment, 22–24, 29
four modes of DBT therapy,
  18–22, 28, 29
four skill modules of DBT
  practice, 7–9
hierarchy of treatment, 20, 122
life worth living as goal, 20, 42,
  121–22, 131–133, 134, 136
pleasant events for
  emotional health, 84
resources, accessing, 25, 142–44
skills plan, putting into
  action, 130
ten primary emotions
  addressed in, 32
Dialectics
  cognitive dysregulation,
    as targeting, 37
  daily life, integrating dialectical
    thinking into, 26
  describing and defining, 4–5, 140
  dialectical statements, 6–7
  dialectical worldview, 13, 15
  three states of mind and, 49–51
Diary Cards
  as a behavior-tracking tool, 23, 41
  daily entries in, 122, 136
  describing and defining, 140
  keeping a diary card, 27, 121
  resources for, 123, 142
  staying focused via, 136
  therapist, reviewing with, 19, 43, 133
Dissociation, 37
Distraction techniques, 65–66
Distress Tolerance
  DBT focus on, 7, 8, 12
  for substance abuse, 13
  SUDs, regulating via, 64, 80, 116

E
Effectiveness skill, 55, 56
Emotional Avoidance, 38, 49, 140

as a DBT module, 7, 9, 93
describing and defining, 9, 101, 139
effectiveness under lower
SUDs, 64, 80
how interpersonal effectiveness
skills work together, 115–16
interpersonal dysregulation, 36, 37
obstacles to interpersonal
effectiveness, 101–104

J

Judgment
DEAR MAN, keeping
judgments out of, 105
emotions, impact of judgments
on, 40, 44, 60
mindfulness, no judgment
in, 48, 51
nonjudgmental practice, 52,
54–55, 91, 100, 110
paying attention, no
judgment during, 108
self-judgment, not engaging
in, 96
Justified Emotion, 90, 140
"Just Say No" program, 123

L

Limbic System, 33, 40
Linehan, Marsha M.
BehavioralTech.org as a
Linehan DBT model, 2
BPD population, creating
treatment for, 12
DBT, as developing, 3, 19, 38, 84, 121
dialectics theory, working with, 3–5
dysregulation, identifying
five areas of, 36
life worth living, focus
on notion of, 131
mindfulness, on skills involved in, 52
problems, on options in
responding to, 18

ten primary emotions,
identifying, 32
triggers, on handling, 68
on Wise Mind ACCEPTS
skill, 65

M

Marx, Karl, 5
Mastery Building, 88
Mindfulness
in DBT program, 3, 12–13, 41, 47, 96
in DEAR MAN exercise, 107
describing and defining, 7–8, 48–49
group exercises, 20, 130
making space for, 58–59
mindful self-soothing, 67
muscle of mindfulness,
building, 58, 60
One-Mindfully exercise, 54, 55
One Thing in the Moment
practice, 74–75
pleasant events, mindful
participation in, 84, 97
STOP method, proceeding
mindfully with, 68–69
SUDs, regulating via, 64,
76, 80, 94, 116
WHAT skills, use in
mindfulness
practice, 52, 100
Wise Mind, accessing
through, 8, 51, 57, 128
Missing Links Analysis, 129
Mood-Dependent Behavior,
42, 57, 95, 102. 140
Motivation
in DBT treatment, 22, 133, 136
increasing motivation to
change, 23
maintaining motivation, 130–31
motivating action, 86
of therapists, 21–22, 24
tips for staying motivated, 134

ACKNOWLEDGMENTS

First and foremost, I would like to acknowledge my son, Finn, for his patience with me while I spent hours at the computer. Thank you, sweetheart. Love and gratitude to my brother, Tom, for emotional support and great barbeque. And thanks to Dana Dixon, Liz Corpstein, Vanessa Campos, Darcy Clark, Bob Connolly, Karen McCrea, and the rest of the team at Village Counseling and Wellness.

ABOUT THE AUTHOR

Suzette Bray, MA, LMFT, is a licensed marriage and family therapist based in Los Angeles California. She is the founder of Village Counseling and Wellness, a program specializing in dialectical behavior therapy (DBT) for adults and teens. It has offices in Burbank and Claremont, California. Suzette is a sought-after speaker and trainer on topics related to emotional health. You can find out more about Suzette at VillageCounselingAndWellness.com.